Matthew

INTERPRETATION
BIBLE STUDIES

Scripture quotations, unless otherwise noted, are from the New Revised Standard Version of the Bible, copyright © 1989 by the Division of Christian Education of the National Council of the Churches of Christ in the U.S.A., and are used by permission.

The photographs on pages 1, 21, 29, 91, and 95 are used by permission of The Fellowship for Readers of the Urantia Book.

The photographs on pages 19, 52, 61, 73 are courtesy of SuperStock, Inc.

The illustration on page 15, *The Adoration of the Shepherds: with the Lamp,* by Rembrandt Harmensz van Rijn, is reproduced by permission of the Fine Arts Museums of San Francisco, the Achenbach Foundation for Graphic Arts, Bruno and Sadie Adriani Collection, 1959.40.24.

Book design by Drew Stevens
Cover design by Pam Poll
Cover illustration Robert Stratton

First edition
Published by Geneva Press
Louisville, Kentucky

This book is printed on acid-free paper that meets the American National Standards Institute Z39.48 standard ♾

PRINTED IN THE UNITED STATES OF AMERICA

00 01 02 03 04 05 06 07 — 10 9 8 7 6 5 4 3 2

Library of Congress Cataloging-in-Publication Data

McKenzie, Alyce M., 1955–
    Matthew / Alyce M. McKenzie.
        p.   cm. — (Interpretation Bible studies)
    Includes bibliographical references.
    ISBN 0-664-50022-6
    1. Bible. N.T. Matthew—Criticism, interpretation, etc.
I. Title.   II. Series.
BS2575.2.M32   1998
226.2′06—dc21   98-11626

Matthew

ALYCE M. MCKENZIE

Geneva Press
Louisville, Kentucky

Contents

Series Introduction

The Bible long has been revered for its witness to God's presence and redeeming activity in the world; its message of creation and judgment, love and forgiveness, grace and hope; its memorable characters and stories; its challenges to human life; and its power to shape faith. For generations people have found in the Bible inspiration and instruction, and, for nearly as long, commentators and scholars have assisted students of the Bible. This series, Interpretation Bible Studies (IBS), continues that great heritage of scholarship with a fresh approach to biblical study.

Designed for ease and flexibility of use for either personal or group study, IBS helps readers not only to learn about the history and theology of the Bible, understand the sometimes difficult language of biblical passages, and marvel at the biblical accounts of God's activity in human life, but also to accept the challenge of the Bible's call to discipleship. IBS offers sound guidance for deepening one's knowledge of the Bible and for faithful Christian living in today's world.

IBS was developed out of three primary convictions. First, the Bible is the church's scripture and stands in a unique place of authority in Christian understanding. Second, good scholarship helps readers understand the truths of the Bible and sharpens their perception of God speaking through the Bible. Third, deep knowledge of the Bible bears fruit in one's ethical and spiritual life.

Each IBS volume has ten brief units of key passages from a book of the Bible. By moving through these units, readers capture the sweep of the whole biblical book. Each unit includes study helps, such as maps, photos, definitions of key terms, questions for reflection, and suggestions for resources for further study. In the back of each volume is a Leader's Guide that offers helpful suggestions on how to use IBS.

The Interpretation Bible Studies series grows out of the well-known Interpretation commentaries (John Knox Press), a series that helps preachers and teachers in their preparation. Although each IBS volume bears a deep kinship to its companion Interpretation commentary, IBS can stand alone. The reader need not be familiar with the Interpretation commentary to benefit from IBS. However, those who want to discover even more about the Bible will benefit by consulting Interpretation commentaries too.

Through the kind of encounter with the Bible encouraged by the Interpretation Bible Studies, the church will continue to discover God speaking afresh in the scriptures.

Introduction to Matthew

The Gospel of Matthew is placed first in the New Testament, not because it was written first, but because of the importance given to this Gospel in the life of the church. Matthew's depiction of Jesus' teachings in the context of his death and resurrection has shone like a moral beacon on the church's path through the centuries. In familiar passages like the Sermon on the Mount (chaps. 5–7) and the Parables Discourse (chap. 13), the Gospel of Matthew offers instruction and encouragement for living a righteous life according to the new righteousness revealed in Christ.

Most people, if they are fortunate, know at least one person they can count on for moral consistency and integrity. They turn to this person in times of trouble and questioning. Throughout the centuries Matthew's Gospel has been just such a stable friend to the church. Christians have known they can turn to Matthew and find an earnestness of guiding moral principles from start to finish. The express purpose of the Gospel was to shape the moral vision and behavior of communities of postresurrection Christians in changing circumstances.

The Sea of Galilee

Matthew's Gospel provides more than ethical guidelines, however. It nourishes contemporary readers with a balanced spiritual diet, announcing the good news of what God has done and is doing in our lives through Christ, to which the ethical life is a response. Matthew presents Jesus as a teacher, but the teachings of Jesus are important to Matthew because of the identity of Jesus: the Messiah, the Son of David, the Son of God—obedient to God unto death and raised by God to undying life.

For further reading about the Gospel of Matthew, see Douglas R. A. Hare, *Matthew*, Interpretation (Louisville, Ky.: John Knox Press, 1993); Thomas G. Long, *Matthew*, Westminster Bible Companion (Louisville, Ky.: Westminster John Knox Press, 1997); William Barclay, *The Gospel of Matthew*, 2 vols., Daily Study Bible (Philadelphia: Westminster Press, 1975).

Matthew wants readers to be motivated to a life of obedience, but not overwhelmed and paralyzed by the rigor of Jesus' moral teachings. He means for us to be awed and grateful, knowing the lengths to which Jesus the teacher will go and the heights to which God will raise him. Therefore, in Matthew the ethical demands appear in the context of the larger story of Jesus. Readers are given hope and courage to live the kingdom life by knowing that Jesus, who calls them to ethical obedience, is the same Jesus who gave his life for the forgiveness of sins and who is present now as risen Savior to give them strength to be obedient and mercy when they fall short.

Author and Situation

We do not know the name of the author of the Gospel of Matthew. Because the material in Matthew does not seem to come from an eyewitness to Jesus' ministry, the author was probably not Matthew the tax collector, one of the disciples of Jesus (Matt. 9:9—for convenience, however, the traditional name "Matthew" is maintained throughout this study). Some scholars have suggested that the author was a Jewish Christian living in about A.D. 85–90 in the Syrian town of Antioch the city from which Paul and Barnabas were sent as missionaries (see Acts 13–14).

Even though we do not know the author's name, we can discern something of the context in which he wrote, because he weaves issues and concerns from his own day into his treatment of the story of Jesus. Indeed, by creatively echoing the experiences of his own readers in the account of Jesus, the members of Matthew's church can see themselves and their needs in the events of Jesus' ministry. To some extent, Jesus, his disciples, and Matthew's readers all become "contemporaries" (Luz, 9).

One concern that reverberates in the pages of Matthew is the tension between the Jewish synagogue and the new Christian community. Scholars have puzzled long over Matthew's ambivalent relationship to Jewish tradition. On the one hand, Matthew is loyal to the Torah (the key scriptures of the Jews), but on the other hand he is sharply critical of its main teachers, the scribes and Pharisees. His Gospel combines penetrating criticisms of their behavior (as in chap. 23), alongside instructions to abide by the Torah, to obey the law even to the last jot and tittle (5:17–19). There is the call to obey the instruction of the scribes and Pharisees, but also the caution to reject their lifestyle (23:2–3). Disciples are expected to keep the Sabbath, to fast, to bring their offerings in accordance with Jewish tradition (6:16ff.; 24:20; 5:23f.), and to pay the Temple tax (17:24ff.), but at the same time, Jesus is presented as the one who challenges traditional interpretations of Sabbath, ritual purity, and food laws. Moreover, many scholars assert that the prolonged attack against "the scribes and Pharisees" in Matthew 23 may reflect more a conflict between Matthew and the rabbis of his own time than an actual contest between Jesus and the Jewish leaders (Perrin, 171).

So what is the relationship in Matthew between the older faith and the new; between synagogue and church? The heritage of Judaism is still powerfully evident in Matthew's language and categories and in what he says about worship and devotional practices, but Matthew repeatedly speaks of "their scribes" and "their synagogues" (7:29; 9:35; 23:34) when speaking about the Jews. Perhaps the Gospel of Matthew was·

Key Terms

Essenes A group of Jews who separated themselves from the larger religious body to become the community of God's new covenant. Essenes practiced communal ownership of property, celibacy, and strict dietary laws.

Pharisees The Gospel portrait is slanted against this group, mostly presenting them as hypocrites and opponents of Jesus. A more accurate portrait shows them to be a priestly group whose heritage might trace back to the lawyers. Often sectarian in their practices, particularly with respect to diet, ritual purity, and Sabbath observance, the Pharisees were well respected as leaders.

Rabbi In the days of Jesus, any learned teacher of the Law (whether ordained or not).

Sadducees An aristocratic, priestly group who believed in the centrality of the Temple and whose views stood opposed to the Pharisees, particularly in disbelieving in angels, the resurrection of the dead, and the validity of the oral tradition of interpreting scripture.

Sanhedrin The ruling body of Jews, composed of chief priests, scribes, and elders, primarily responsible for making judgments and collecting the Temple tax.

Scribes Originally a purely secular office whose function was that of lawyers, interpreters, and copyists of the Torah. In time they came to have more religious standing and were associated with the Pharisees.

Zealots A group of Jews, with strong nationalistic tendencies, who opposed the Roman occupation of Palestine.

written to a church that had once been a part of the synagogue but had now broken with the Jewish community. Maybe Matthew's church was a Jewish-Christian congregation that had begun to incorporate Gentile, or non-Jewish, members. This might explain why much in Matthew comes from Judaism; but at the same time, the author presents the church as a radical departure from the old ways (Hill, 40–41). Matthew calls the church to be both faithful to its Jewish roots and responsive to the new vision proclaimed by Jesus, to be like the "wise scribe" portrayed by Jesus, "trained for the kingdom of heaven . . . , who brings out of his treasure what is new and what is old" (13:52).

Matthew's church not only struggled with its Jewish heritage but also wrestled with its new mission to the Gentile world. For example, stories like the visit of the Gentile "wise men" to worship the Jewish Messiah (2:1–12) may well reflect the challenge that Matthew's own church was facing in receiving Gentile worshipers. Matthew understood Jesus to be the Messiah for all people, Jew and Gentile alike.

We also can sense some of the internal circumstances in Matthew's church. For example, in the miracles and healings of Jesus we find reflections of some of the needs of Matthew's congregation. Jesus gives sight to the blind (9:27–31; 12:22–24; 20:29–34; 21:14); he forgives the sins of the lame (9:6); he praises the faith of those in desperate need (8:5–13; 9:20–22, 27–31; 17:20–21); and he feeds the hungry (14:13–21; 15:32–39). In the midst of Matthew's church were those who needed to come from the blinding darkness of an old age into the shining light of the new. In his

Key Terms

What's the difference?

synagogue A gathering place for worship. Many communities had synagogues.

tabernacle A sacred tent, a type of portable sanctuary. During earlier times in the Jews' history, the Ark of the Covenant was kept in a tabernacle.

Temple Located in Jerusalem, the official site for the worship of God. Destroyed and rebuilt a number of times, the Temple was viewed as a symbol of the nation of Israel and of God's enduring presence with them as a chosen people. As long as the Temple stood, all was safe.

What did people expect from a Messiah?

In the time of Jesus there was a complex mixture of understandings about who the Messiah would be and what he would do. Primarily there were two strands of thought. The first strand was that the Messiah would be a descendant of David and would rule brilliantly over a new Israel in a blessed era of peace. The second strand was more in line with the reference in Daniel to a Son of Man, an otherworldly being who coexisted with God and would return at the end of this age to pass judgment. The concept of a Messiah who would suffer was completely unknown to the contemporaries of Jesus.

4

midst were those who needed to have their sins forgiven. In his midst were the needy whose faith drove them to Jesus. In his midst were the spiritually hungry who needed to be nourished by the Bread of Life. The miracles of Jesus inspire believers, strengthened by the presence of the risen Lord, to nourish the faith of others.

Today, as in Matthew's time, churches attempt to reach out to other groups as the generations roll on and neighborhoods change, and, sometimes there is resistance to that outreach. Matthew's church, like today's, had its share of people whose refrain was "This is our church; who are these new people who are trying to change things?" His church had its share of lukewarm Christians, something like the one-hour-a-week Christians of today. His church, like today's, had its back-row worshipers, barely present and poised for flight. Somewhere in Matthew's church we find ourselves; Matthew's story is our story.

Matthew's Theological Vision

Matthew, in dialogue with both Jews and Gentiles of his day, emphasizes active faith as the core of discipleship. He insists on the church's openness to people of all races and of varying backgrounds. To those alert to the Jewish roots of the church, Matthew emphasizes Jesus' lineage from David, his fulfillment of the Hebrew Scriptures and his commitment to the teachings of the Law and the Prophets.

Matthew wants to remind his Gentile readers that even though they do not have to adhere to ritual and dietary laws, they still have ethical obligations that come as an outflow of faith. Paying lip service to Jesus is not enough. Those who hear without doing are like those who build houses on sand when a rainstorm is on the way (7:24–27). To drive this point home, Matthew concludes the Sermon on the Mount with this warning: "Not everyone who says to me, 'Lord, Lord,' will enter the kingdom of heaven, but only the one who does the will of my Father in heaven" (7:21).

Matthew's Jesus called Jewish and Gentile Christians alike to a righteousness that exceeds that of the scribes and Pharisees (5:20). Righteousness is not a mechanical obedience to rules or creative rationalizations of what we are already doing. Righteousness is an inward faithfulness and obedience to the spirit of the law of God: love of God and love of neighbor (22:39–40). Sometimes referred to as superior, or higher, righteousness, "genuine righteousness" (or "active righteousness") is a major theme in Matthew. Righteousness is not the possession only of the spiritual elite; active righteousness should be a quality of *all* Christians, linking purity within to a passion for justice toward others. Genuine righteousness is reflected in a life of service; it is not just something to which we pay lip service (15:8). As the parable of the sower suggests, righteousness means hearing, doing, and bearing fruit (13:18–23).

Who demonstrates this kind of righteousness? It cannot be inherited; it must spring from faith. Matthew condemns the attitude of those who believed descent from Abraham guaranteed their salvation. Nor is righteousness the product of wealth or power. Even with all their riches and influence, people like Pilate or Herod lacked the spiritual fortitude of comparatively powerless individuals like Joseph or Pilate's wife (Levine, 252ff.). Those who demonstrate active righteousness in response to God's gracious invitation to relationship have in common their recognition that they need God. In Jesus' own words, "Those who are well have no need of a physician, but those who are sick" (9:12). In reality, we all need the divine physician, but those less cushioned by material comfort and status seem more likely to keep the doctor's appointment.

> ## Want to Know More?
>
> **About leading Bible study groups?** See Roberta Hestenes, *Using the Bible in Groups* (Philadelphia: Westminster Press, 1983).
>
> **About the development of the Gospels?** See William M. Ramsay, *The Westminster Guide to the Books of the Bible* (Louisville, Ky.: Westminster John Knox Press, 1994), 289–316; John Barton, *How the Bible Came to Be* (Louisville, Ky.: Westminster John Knox Press, 1997), 18–22, 44–46; Archibald M. Hunter, *Introducing the New Testament*, 3d rev. ed. (Philadelphia: Westminster Press, 1972), 23–26.
>
> **About the content or themes of each Gospel?** See Duncan S. Ferguson, *Bible Basics: Mastering the Content of the Bible* (Louisville, Ky.: Westminster John Knox Press, 1995), 57–65; Hunter, *Introducing the New Testament*, 37–70.
>
> **About messianic expectations?** See Celia Brewer Marshall, *A Guide through the New Testament* (Louisville, Ky.: Westminster John Knox Press, 1994), 33.

Matthew's vision of ethical living applies to both our private lives and the life of the church. He is concerned about the church's way of life in response to the message of Jesus. His goal is to strengthen and guide the community to be the church obedient. He locates the church within the context of Israel's salvation history, shaping his material to emphasize three truths about its identity and purpose. First, the church is the true Israel, replacing the old Israel in the center of God's purpose. Second, the church in the present age is a mixed body, including both worthy and unworthy, wheat and weeds (13:24–30) among its members. Third, the church is called to live a new and more exacting way of righteousness, and the foundation for this new way of life is laid in Jesus' Sermon on the Mount (see study units 3 and 4).

1

Matthew 1:1–25

The Lineage, Birth, and Naming of Jesus Christ

Who is Jesus Christ? This question serves as a beacon to all who struggle to be faithful to his memory, alert to his presence in their lives, and open to the future to which he beckons. The question of Jesus' identity runs like a scarlet cord through the whole Gospel of Matthew. It is raised in the very first verse, unwinds gradually through the Gospel narrative, and comes to a bold climax in the final scene, often called the Great Commission (28:18–20). There, at the end, Jesus is clearly seen as Lord, the true Son of God. He claims "all authority in heaven and on earth," sends the disciples to make new disciples in his name, and promises to be with them "to the end of the age."

The issue of Jesus' identity is crucial for all who read Matthew's Gospel because our own identity is caught up in his. To recognize that Jesus is "Lord" is to become a disciple. To know who Jesus is and to call him "Lord" is to acknowledge Jesus' living authority over every aspect of life—personal, relational, political, economic—and to join his mission to the world.

The Genealogy

Matthew opens his Gospel by naming Jesus as "Messiah," or "Christ," a term that means "anointed" (1:1). Matthew announces to his readers that Jesus is God's anointed one, a divine agent sent on a holy mission by God; in Matthew's mind, "Messiah" is basically equivalent to another title for Jesus: "Son of God." Indeed, "Messiah" and "Son of God" appear together in two pivotal passages: Peter's confession (16:16) and the high priest's accusation (26:63).

For Christians today, to call Jesus the "Christ" and "the Son of God" seems obvious, taken for granted—almost as if "Jesus Christ" were his first and last names. But in the earliest days of the Christian church, there was no such obvious link. How did a carpenter's son named Jesus from an ordinary family in the ordinary village of Nazareth come to be called "Messiah" and "Son of God"? Matthew begins his answer to this question by unfolding Jesus' family tree or genealogy. At first glance, this seems like a deadly dull way to start an account of an exciting life. We are tempted to skip over the genealogy and get to the real action of Jesus' ministry. But Matthew includes the genealogy for good reason—to make three important affirmations about Jesus' identity.

In the first place, Matthew includes the genealogy to show that Jesus—though he may seem to the world like an ordinary man—is in fact a king, "the son of David," a legitimate descendant of the royal line. Second, Matthew demonstrates that Jesus was in every sense an authentic Jew, "the son of Abraham." "Messiah" was first and foremost a Jewish term, the one in whom the hopes of Israel were fulfilled. Matthew traces Jesus' heritage all the way back to the very beginning of the Jewish people—to Abraham, Isaac, and Jacob. As "the son of David, the son of Abraham," Jesus stood in continuity with the great Jewish tradition, the history and legacy of Israel.

Matthew's third reason for including the genealogy is to show that in Jesus the Messiah,

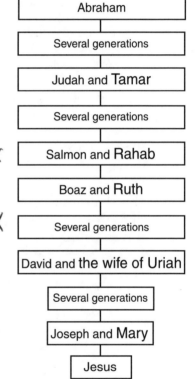

The Genealogy of Jesus

God makes a new beginning. In Jesus Christ, we participate in that new beginning, regardless of our former religious background. This affirmation is conveyed in Matthew's use of the word "genealogy" (Greek *genesis*), which Matthew chose to make the connection in readers' minds with the first book of the Hebrew Scriptures, where "in the beginning . . . God created the heavens and the earth" (Gen. 1:1). In Jesus, God provides a "new Genesis."

The Best Antiques are Old Friends

What can we learn from the genealogy in Matthew? There are several insights to be gleaned:

1. Jesus is an expression of (the old,) an embodiment of the time-honored traditions, the long history of faith, and the ancient hopes of Israel. He is the Messiah whom the Hebrews have been expecting through the centuries. Faith in, and obedience to, Jesus is a fulfillment, not a denial, of the heritage of Israel. Later, in the Sermon on the Mount, Jesus will say, "Do not think that I have come to abolish the law or the prophets; I have come not to abolish but to fulfill" (5:17).

> "All history is in God's hands; since the election of Abraham, history has been moving toward Jesus as its goal."
> —Eduard Schweizer, *The Good News according to Matthew*, 24.

Not only does this continuity with the past underscore the steadfastness of God; it also underscores the urgency of ethical response to the gospel. In some church circles these days, a formula for church growth is being promoted that, in short, emphasizes only God's love and acceptance over and against God's demand for righteousness. "Soft-pedal the cross and Jesus' call to sacrifice and ethical rigor. Meet people's needs and expectations. Market what the church can do for them." Theologian Dietrich Bonhoeffer, in his exposition of the Sermon on the Mount titled *The Cost of Discipleship,* called this theology "cheap grace":

> Cheap grace is the grace we bestow on ourselves . . . the preaching of forgiveness without requiring repentance, baptism without church discipline, Communion without confession. Cheap grace is grace without discipleship. . . . Costly grace is the gospel which must be sought again and again, the gift which must be asked for, the door at which a man must knock. . . . It is costly because it costs a man his life, and it is grace because it gives a man the only true life, (Bonhoeffer, 36–37)

2. However, Jesus is also an expression of *the new and unexpected.* We see this in the fact that the names of four women whose stories are told in the Old Testament are included in the genealogy, and not the four we might expect. We find not Sarah, Rebecca, Rachel, and Leah, but Tamar, Rahab, the wife of Uriah (Bathsheba), and Ruth. Including women would have been surprising in itself, but less so if the women who made the cut were four respectable matriarchs. Instead, Matthew includes four women, at least two of them Gentiles, whose backgrounds and actions in some respects might be better left as skeletons in the family closet!

10

Why? Some interpreters have suggested that Matthew's purpose is simply to show that God's plan of salvation includes Gentiles. This may be so, but it is more likely that Matthew intended his readers to see these women as positive examples of the surprising ways God works in history. These women showed strong and aggressive faith despite their social powerlessness. Matthew elsewhere shows an affinity for portraying women who demonstrate bold initiative; for example, the Canaanite woman (15:21ff.) and the woman who touches the fringe of Jesus' cloak (9:22). Three of the four women he includes in his genealogy are women of just such courageous action! Tamar claims her rights when Judah neglects them (Genesis 38); Rahab recognizes the power of the Hebrew God and so protects the scouts (Joshua 2); Ruth, following Naomi's advice, moves Boaz to action (Ruth 3).

In the ancient world, women were often forced to employ manipulative, behind-the-scenes tactics because society accorded them little influence through accepted public channels (Camp, 140). Tamar, Rahab, and Ruth use cunning, a sort of unconventional wisdom to wring justice from unjust events. Matthew's message is that God uses those on society's sidelines to advance the plan of salvation. Faithful actions, not inherited political or religious status, or habit, place one in the Savior's family tree. The women in the genealogy, along with other biblical women like Esther, the Wise Woman of Tekoa, and Abigail are, according to Claudia Camp, "women who take initiative on God's behalf by indirect means" (Camp, 137). By acting in ways that challenged the expectations of their times, these women advanced God's plan. The genealogy implies that with ancestors like this, Jesus will too. With a Savior like Jesus, we can too (Levine, 253).

> "If Matthew had ransacked the pages of the Old Testament for improbable candidates he could not have discovered four more incredible ancestors for Jesus Christ." —William Barclay, *The Gospel of Matthew,* Daily Study Bible, vol. 1, p. 17.

In the listing of the genealogy, Jesus is a blend of the old and the new, the traditional and the unexpected. For those of Jewish heritage, Matthew employs the genealogy to call them to be faithful to their religious roots and traditions but also open to the new, to recognize that being a descendant of Abraham means acting out one's faith, not just unrolling one's religious pedigree: "My family has belonged to this church for fifty years. My grandfather gave the money for the steeple!" Discipleship makes a claim on our actions as well as our words.

As for his Gentile readers, Matthew calls on them also to integrate the old and the new. As for the new, the message of the genealogy is that Gentiles have been incorporated into God's saving purpose and should be welcomed into the household of faith. A new church member once told her pastor, "I was not raised in the church but came to a point in my life when I felt drawn to give it a try. The first Sunday I visited your church, I arrived a little late. Everyone was already singing the first hymn. Lots of people weren't even looking at their hymnals—they already knew the words. I panicked and froze behind one of the pillars in the narthex, unsure as to whether I really wanted to go in. Was I dressed well enough? How would I know when to stand up and when to sit down? How would I be accepted by all these pillars of the community?"

Some of the Gentiles in Matthew's church no doubt felt like latecomers to the faith, knocking on the door of an exclusive club whose preferred members were former Jews. Matthew's message, both to the people behind the pillar and to the pillars in the pews, is that the invitation is to Gentiles as well as to Jews.

Both Gentiles and Jews must accept God's gracious and joyful invitation, not with a phone call or token gift, but by leading righteous lives. For both groups, faithful actions in response to Jesus make one a disciple, not inherited religious status or lip service. The one-sided, cheap-grace view of God's good news in Christ was present in Matthew's day, too. In part, Matthew wrote his Gospel as a reaction against the cheap-grace viewpoint. His Gospel emphasizes a distinct way of individual and communal life that flows from faith in Jesus. The life of genuine righteousness has everything to do with joy, but it is a joy that springs from commitment and rigorous discipline in life.

3. The genealogy also shows *the will and power of God to wring redemption out of human sinfulness.* This may well be behind the mention of the Babylonian exile ("the deportation to Babylon," 1:12), which the prophets saw as judgment upon the people for their sin (see Jeremiah 32), and the somewhat puzzling reference to Bathsheba ("the wife of Uriah," 1:6). In the biblical story of her involvement with David (2 Samuel 11), Bathsheba does not seem to embody the same decisive action as the other women named in the genealogy. Indeed, the account is mum as to her feelings and motives. Perhaps her inclusion in the genealogy is more about divine action than human action, acknowledging that God can bring good even from corrupt, sin-ridden situations. David was a great man of

12

strength who also had times of great weakness. God turned even those flawed moments into redemption. Out of the union of David and Bathsheba came Solomon, a forebear of Jesus. From David's lineage came an even greater king who taught and lived a righteousness that gained power by self-giving rather than by grasping. The inclusion of "the wife of Uriah" in the genealogy of Jesus demonstrates that there is hope for all of us who become embroiled in circumstances that bring pain to others and self-loathing to our own souls. God is a master weaver whose skilled, gracious hands can weave the saddest, most sordid scenes from our life stories into the tapestry of divine salvation.

Joseph's Role

Matthew moves immediately from the genealogy to the story of Joseph, and the flow from one to the other makes sense. In Joseph's story we see lived out much of what we discovered in the genealogy—the tension between the old and the new, between traditional forms of righteousness and the surprising righteousness of God's kingdom. Joseph is a righteous man, a descendant of David, and represents all that is good about the heritage of Israel. In Matthew's account of Jesus' miraculous conception, Joseph discerns the new thing that God is doing and responds to it in obedience. In doing so, he embodies active righteousness.

In the Gospel of Luke, Mary is the primary human actor in the story of Jesus' birth. The focus is on her modeling a passive acceptance of what is happening to her ("Let it be with me according to your word," Luke 1:38). Matthew selects Joseph as his leading actor to highlight the active component in our human response to God. Joseph never speaks a word in the Gospel, but his action is crucial to God's work of salvation through Jesus.

Matthew is clear about what Joseph's role is *not*. He is not the biological father of Jesus. The child is conceived by the Holy Spirit. This is by no means the Spirit's only appearance in the Gospel. The Spirit appears at crucial junctures throughout the Gospel. For example, the Spirit reappears to affirm Jesus' divine role (3:16–17), to drive him into the wilderness to be tested by Satan (4:1), to give him power (12:28), and to test believers for entry into the age to come (12:32). The Spirit seems to act in two capacities: to test and challenge those who are in their comfort zones, and to confirm instances

A. to TesT + challenge

B. To confirm Active faithfulness

13

of active faithfulness. We would do well today to be sensitive to the Spirit's workings in the depths of our lives in both capacities.

Matthew explains the miraculous conception as the prophetic fulfillment of Isaiah 7:14. The Hebrew version of Isaiah states simply that a "young woman" has conceived, but the Greek version, which Matthew follows, translates the term for young woman as *parthenos,* or virgin. Isaiah's original reference was probably to a young woman, or virgin, who would conceive a child in the normal manner after her marriage. Christian interpreters read this verse as a prediction of Jesus' birth. Because sometimes Israel is called a virgin in the Hebrew Scriptures (2 Kings 19:21; Isa. 37:22; Amos 5:2), Matthew may view Mary as a representative of the nation of Israel. His idea may be that Virgin Israel cannot bring forth the Messiah without God's direct intervention.

> "Therefore the Lord himself will give you a sign. Look, the young woman is with child and shall bear a son, and shall name him Immanuel." —Isaiah 7:14

Matthew interprets Jesus' conception as happening, not by the natural process of procreation, but by the direct will of God. Vital to God's plan is for Jesus to be born into the family of David and to be accepted as a part of that family. For the plan to succeed, Joseph must play an active, irreplaceable role. Joseph must agree to be the father to a child who is not his. He must summon faith sufficient to commit a crucial act of incorporation. At the urging of the angel, he must accept Jesus as his son and give him a name to seal the relationship. God's miraculous action in causing the pregnancy will be incomplete without the incorporation of the child into Joseph's family.

> "Joseph becomes . . . a model for the Christian life. He learns that being truly righteous does not mean looking up a rule in a book and then doing the 'right thing'; it means wrestling with the complexities of a problem, listening for the voice of God, and then doing God's thing." —Thomas G. Long, *Matthew,* Westminster Bible Companion, 14.

✳ As disciples we are called, not to make miracles happen on our own steam, but to allow them to happen by cooperating actively with God's grace. This is Joseph's role—to allow the miracle to happen by accepting the child into his family and naming him as his own. Mary apparently is guilty of fornication, and by religious obligation Joseph should annul the marriage (Deut. 22:23–24). To enable the miracle, God must encourage Joseph to forsake this level of righteousness for another. Instead of following conventional religious practice, God will lead Joseph in a new way.

Using his own best wisdom of what God's will requires, tempered with compassion, Joseph decides to annul the marriage to Mary, but to do so secretly to avoid humiliating her in public. Joseph's own understanding of faithfulness presents an obstacle to the plan of God. As night falls, God acts to remove this obstacle. An angel is sent to convince Joseph to accept his new God-intended role.

The terse narrative doesn't give a clue as to the anguish the young groom-to-be must have felt, but we can empathize with him out of experiences we have had of betrayal and disappointment by others. We leave Joseph tossing and turning in his tortured sleep and flash forward to the night of Jesus' birth. Our imaginations are helped by a famous painting of the manger scene by Rembrandt. Though based on Luke's story of the shepherds' visit, nonetheless the painting shows the young Joseph, hair tousled, face lined with fatigue and strain,

The Adoration of the Shepherds: with the Lamp.
Etching by Rembrandt Harmensz van Rijn, c. 1654.
Fine Arts Museums of San Francisco

standing with one shoulder thrust forward as if to protect Mary from the throng, and gazing into the fire with an anxious look. Between his decision to divorce her and his presence at her side on that night of birthing, something dramatic must have happened. What caused this change?

Our text tells us—a night of birthing just as real as Christmas Eve. The birth of an earthly father for the Son of God. In his sleeping state, Joseph allows God to speak to the depths of his heart and to propose a resolution to the dilemma that his human reason had failed to discern. On this night, an angel hovered near, whispering a message from God to Joseph. The angel addressed him as "son of David," a clue that his role in the story has to do with his Davidic descent. We may imagine the conversation: "Believe her unbelievable story," whispered the angel. "Marry her, accept this child into your family, and become the father of God's child."

"He will need a father as he grows to manhood, not just any father, but one like you, one who will teach him to take risks like the one you are about to take, for he will be tempted not to take them.

He will need a father like you to teach him to withstand the disapproval of others, as you will soon have to withstand it.

He will need a father like you to teach him what to do in situations like this one, when all hope seems lost and only pain remains, and to model how to believe the unbelievable good news and to walk ahead in faith.

If you do not walk the hard road to Bethlehem, who will teach him how to climb the cruel hill to Calvary?"

And, as Matthew tells us, "when Joseph awoke from sleep, he did as the angel of the Lord commanded him" (1:24).

For Matthew, active deeds of righteousness are an integral part of faithfulness. Joseph is an example of the genuine, active righteousness Matthew commends. Like the others mentioned in the genealogy, Joseph acted in a manner not expected by the social mores of his times. Joseph acted to further divine purposes, and so will Jesus. Joseph and the others were relatively powerless people, but in Matthew's Gospel they appear in a flattering light compared with the religious and political power brokers of Jesus' day: Caiaphas, Herod, and Pilate. Joseph acted out of mercy in the cause of justice, not out of ritual obedience in the cause of conventional piety (Levine, 254). Joseph's motive was to cooperate in channeling the power of God, not to preserve or pile up personal power.

Here is a poor man of tremendous dignity. Here is a man whose trade is to create useful, beautiful things with his hands. Here is a man for whom actions speak louder than words. Here is a man willing to give God the last word. Here is a man capable of directing his son and his son's followers in paths of steady, daily obedience to God without counting the cost. Here is a man who chose to be present for his son; he modeled God's choice to be present in Jesus. By his own obe-

---

Want to Know More?

About angels? See Paul J. Achtemeier, *Harper's Bible Dictionary* (San Francisco: Harper & Row, 1985), 30.

About understanding the portrayal of women in the Bible? See Carol A. Newsom and Sharon H. Ringe, eds., *Women's Bible Commentary,* expanded ed. (Louisville, Ky.: Westminster John Knox Press, 1998), 251–59, 482–88. For a more technical treatment, see Gail Corrington Streete, *The Strange Woman: Power and Sex in the Bible* (Louisville, Ky.: Westminster John Knox Press, 1997); for an excellent, very readable treatment, see (if available) Evelyn and Frank Stagg, *Woman in the World of Jesus* (Philadelphia: Westminster Press, 1978).

dience to God's plan, Joseph allowed his son to fulfill the mission implied in the name revealed to Joseph by the angel: Emmanuel, God is with us (1:23).

? Questions for Reflection

1. The genealogy in Matthew lists the ancestors of Jesus and conveys the truth that God works through the generations. Who are some of those people, literally and figuratively, who have been your "ancestors" in the faith?
2. The listing of the genealogy of Jesus speaks to ways God has worked in history to bring about God's purposes in people's lives. What are some events in your life that have shown God's handiwork?
3. The genealogy and the story of Joseph disclose the tension in the Christian faith between the old and the new. On the one hand, Jesus was "something old," a "son of David and Abraham," a fulfillment of the traditions, the heritage, and the wisdom of the past. On the other hand, he was "something new," a departure from the expected patterns. How do you see this tension between the old and the new being experienced in the church today? What guidance do you think Matthew provides for this tension?
4. What does it mean to be righteous? Some of those mentioned in Jesus' genealogy (especially the women) didn't follow the accepted ethical practices of their day but were counted righteous in God's eyes. Joseph is called righteous, but God changed his mind about what was the right thing to do. How would you define true righteousness? What are some of the situations today that call for this kind of righteousness?

2 Matthew 3:13–4:11

The Baptism and Testing of the Messiah

Identity
Faithfulness
Call to
Righteousness

Between Joseph's incorporation of the unborn child into his royal family and Jesus' baptism, several key events occur. Each emphasizes Jesus' unique identity, God's faithfulness, and our call to righteousness. Three Gentile astrologers travel dusty roads to kneel at tiny feet (2:1–12), with gifts that point symbolically to aspects of Jesus' identity: royalty (gold), worship (frankincense), and impending death (myrrh). A jealous king greets the Gentile strangers and twitches with hatred because he knows full well who this child is; he knows that his nemesis has come at last.

In the Holy Family's flight and Herod's slaughter of infant boys (2:13–18) we are reminded of the exodus of the people of Israel from Egypt. As readers, we are encouraged to view Jesus' birth in continuity with God's prior acts of liberation from bondage. In John the Baptist's warning that being born into the faith is not to be equated with faithfulness, we hear a harbinger of the first words of Jesus' public ministry: "Repent, for the kingdom of heaven has come near" (4:17).

The Baptism of Jesus

Matthew's Gospel is a process that gradually unfolds an answer to the question "Who is Jesus Christ?" Understanding the identity of Jesus helps shape our own identity, both as communities and individuals. In the story of Jesus' baptism, more is revealed about Jesus' identity as Messiah, and in the temptation account, we see that identity severely tested.

18

The account of Jesus' baptism opens with the portrayal of John the Baptist, who was engaging in the practice of baptism in the wilderness of Judea. The members of the Qumran community, a group of separatist ascetics in Jesus' day, practiced a ritual of washing, which was repeated periodically as a symbolic cleansing from recent sin. By contrast, John's baptism with water for repentance seems to

The Jordan River

have been a "once-and-for-all" ritual. Those who responded to John's preaching and repented were baptized by him, and joined a faithful remnant who believed in a swift end of fiery judgment for the world.

Much end-time speculation and writing of that time focused on a coming new order that God would initiate. The judgment would be preceded by a time of natural disasters. Then the righteous would participate in the kingdom of God, whereas the unrighteous would be consigned to condemnation. John taught that people should purify themselves by his baptism of water now so that they would be cleansed and ready to pass safely through the fires of judgment that were to come.

> **What was striking about John's baptism?** "Baptism was for sinners, and no Jew ever conceived of himself as a sinner shut out from God." —William Barclay, *The Gospel of Matthew*, Daily Study Bible, vol. 1, p. 60.

Given this as a purpose for John's baptism, why would a sinless Jesus be baptized? This question continues to puzzle scholars. Matthew's concern with the identity of Jesus suggests a connection. Matthew alone of the four Gospels includes a dialogue between Jesus and John where John clearly states that Jesus' righteousness is superior to John's. (The role of John the Baptist in relation to Jesus was a much-discussed topic in the church of the first century, with followers of John the Baptist insisting on his precedence over Jesus.) "I need to be baptized by you, and do you come to me?" (3:14). Jesus answers the puzzled John in this way: "Let it be so now; for it is proper for us in this way to fulfill all righteousness" (3:15). A paraphrase of that verse might well be "It

WORD + DEED

is required that you and I fulfill God's will by allowing me to be baptized" (Hare, 21).

Jesus submits to baptism because he is a certain kind of Messiah: a Messiah in deed, not just in word. His submitting to baptism for sin foreshadows his acceptance of the cross. This is a Messiah who does more than express empathy for our painful, sinful human condition. He enters into it, identifying fully with the consequences and remedies. He conscrates himself to his messianic vocation by joining the sinful multitude in the waters of the Jordan. Thereby Jesus himself becomes our premier model in the righteousness that combines faith with action.

> "I like to consider this Jesus' first miracle: the miracle of his humility. . . . It is well known that Jesus ended his career on a cross between thieves; it deserves to be as well known that he began his ministry in a river among penitent sinners." —Frederick Dale Bruner, *Matthew,* vol. 1, p. 83.

On a not too distant day from this one, Jesus will fulfill his risky vocation by a baptism into the waters of death.

Immediately after his baptism there comes the visible conferral of the Holy Spirit accompanied by the words of the heavenly voice: "This is my Son, the Beloved, with whom I am well pleased" (3:17). Matthew's account of this differs from Mark's. Mark depicts the coming of the Spirit and voice from heaven as a private experience of Jesus. In Matthew's version, a combination of quotations from Psalm 2:7 and Isaiah 42:1 is addressed to onlookers. The first half of the divine address is reminiscent of Psalm 2:7, where the king of Israel is addressed as the Son of God, the one who rules in God's stead. The second half of the statement comes from Isaiah 42:1, where God speaks to Israel as the servant people of God, yielded up for the redemption of all the nations: "Here is my servant, whom I uphold, my chosen, in whom my soul delights." This Messiah is not what was expected, but is instead a Servant King.

Some have misinterpreted this moment as the moment Jesus becomes the Messiah, as if all that has led up to this moment has been a prolonged period of probation. For Matthew, Jesus is already Messiah at his conception by the agency of the Holy Spirit. His baptism becomes a high moment of commitment and consecration. Here at the Jordan, Jesus commits himself to his messianic task and receives a sign of an existing divine approval, the visible consecration and empowerment of the Holy Spirit.

In our own baptism, through the Holy Spirit, we partake of the presence of this Savior, who enters fully into the pain and joy of the human condition. This Savior is both committed and able to cleanse us from sin and strengthen us to grow in grace. At the Jordan, the Holy Spirit's power is revealed, which will enable Jesus to withstand the temptations that are about to come to him. The same power of the Holy Spirit strengthens us to withstand temptations today.

IDENTITY OF JESUS + Role of the Spirit

The Temptation

The narrative continues to explore two key issues raised in the baptismal account—the identity of Jesus as Son of God and the role of the Spirit. The temptation narrative suggests that Jesus the Son is one whose identity is tested and forged in the wilderness. By implication we are to understand that the same is true for us as his followers. The temptation narrative builds on the baptismal narrative. Whereas the baptism story asserts Jesus' identity as the Son of God, the temptation account delves into the question, What does it mean to call Jesus the Son of God? Only by continually calling on Jesus the Son of God can we, his disciples, withstand the temptations that face us. A clue to this purpose lies in the fact that the first two temptations begin with the phrase "Since you are the Son of God." (The NRSV has "If you are the Son of God ..." but the former is more in keeping with the purpose of the passage. Satan is not trying to *decide* Jesus' identity. He knows who Jesus is. Satan is trying to get Jesus to *betray* that identity.) Jesus doesn't earn

"The temptations Jesus encountered are not his alone; they are his, of course, but they are also the temptations of all God's people." —Thomas G. Long, *Matthew*, Westminster Bible Companion, 36.

the title "Son of God" by his determined faithfulness. He demonstrates how the Son of God acts amid temptation. Readers of Matthew's Gospel, as individuals and as churches, are urged and empowered by the same Holy Spirit to act in like manner.

The temptation narrative, in its conversation between Jesus and Satan, takes the form of a rabbinical controversy and might reflect an attempt on the part of the early church to clarify the understanding of Jesus' role as Messiah. Jesus' experience is cast in terms of Israel's temptations in the wilderness. Whereas Israel (called "son" by God in Hos. 11:1 and "child" in Deut. 8:5) failed all three tests, Jesus passes them with flying colors and takes upon himself the fulfillment of Israel's destiny. The forty days and forty nights remind us of both Moses' fast (Ex. 34:28, Deut. 9:9, 18; and perhaps Ex. 24:18; see also the fast of Elijah in 1 Kings 19:4–8) and Israel's forty-year wilderness sojourn.

The fifth-century mystics viewed the wilderness as a place for a prophetic challenge to an increasingly wealthy church. Henri J. M. Nouwen describes the role of desert solitude in people's lives this way: "Solitude is the place of the great struggle and the great encounter—the struggle against the compulsions of the false self, and the encounter with the loving God who offers himself as the substance of the new self" (Nouwen, 26). Earlier Nouwen says: "Solitude is the furnace of transformation. Without solitude, we remain a victim of society and continue to wrestle with the illusions of the false self." Jesus himself entered into this furnace. There he was tempted with the three compulsions of the world: to be relevant ('turn stones into loaves'), to be spectacular ('throw yourself down'), and to be powerful ('I will give you all these kingdoms')" (25).

Although a lengthy absence from the daily routine is not always feasible, sometimes a day can be set apart as a retreat or wilderness day. Intentional space in the middle of our hectic lives can allow both the challenge of God to be heard through the temptations we face, and the strength in Christ to name and overcome those temptations. A keynote speaker at an Advent Day Apart for pastors began his sermon with these words: "I must confess that, like all of you, I am too busy to be here." Everyone there agreed, but at the end of a day of prayer, song, and worship, twenty pastors left energized for the tasks of the weeks ahead; they were glad to have been there.

Sometimes life thrusts us into a wilderness where both testing and strengthening occur. Author Madeleine L'Engle once confided in a fan and friend that her best work had come out of times of pain. He responded, "Then, Madam, I wish you a year of suffering!" He was joking, of course. Even God does not wish suffering upon us. But in times of adversity and challenge, God's presence can assure us and strengthen our identity as we face our particular temptations. Then our firsthand experience of God's presence offers good news meant for sharing.

Who is the tempter? Called Satan in Hebrew, the devil (*diabolos*) in Greek, we imagine this figure stalking the pages of the Bible, seeming to grow in hostility and power over against God. The Hebrew faith attributed both good and evil to God's agency. The Satan (adversary) makes cameo appearances as an agent of God in the Old Testament. His primary role was to uncover the weaknesses of humans who were highly regarded by God, allegedly to preserve God's honor (Job 1:6–12; Zech. 3:1–2). Satan becomes increasingly hostile and harmful in later Jewish views of his identity and role. He interferes with God's relationship to Israel through temptation (1 Chron. 21:1), by accusation before God (Zech. 3:1), and by disrupting the course of events throughout Israel's history. His efforts may be defended by good choices, human merit, angelic assistance, or even by God (Kittel and Friedrich, 151).

Gradually, Satan's identity shifts from divine employee to God's chief competitor, in part as the result of Persian influence on Judaism. In that belief system, world history was viewed as a cosmic struggle between the forces of good and light, and those of evil and darkness, with each represented by various angelic or demonic beings. Satan becomes the force of evil in the world. All sorts of extant legends and images about evil stick to Satan as if he were a snowball rolling down a hill. So Satan, then, is associated with the serpent of paradise, an ancient dragon, an exalted angel expelled from heaven, and the evil impulse that resides within each of us (Gen. 4:7).

By the time Jesus meets Satan in the wilderness, the clear understanding is that though he is no longer working for God, he is still up to his old tempter tricks. His apparent motive is to test Jesus to see if he is worthy of the messianic mission. In reality, Satan is seeking to persuade Jesus to betray that mission and side with the kingdom of this world. In the Gospels, the present time is viewed as a showdown between God's rule as inaugurated by Jesus, and that of Satan. The temptation of Jesus exemplifies that showdown.

God's rule or kingdom is a central theme of Jesus' ministry. Matthew prefers the term "kingdom of heaven," heaven being a reverent synonym for God that reflects the Jewish preference for not using the name of God directly (Argyle, 10). Jews of Jesus' day believed that God's reign was eternal (Ps. 145:13) and universal (Ps. 103:19), but only partially recognized on earth. The kingdom was not geographical, but rather a gathering of people obedient to God's will. God already was king by right, but because many did not recognize or obey God's sovereignty, the reign of God was not yet universal in reality. The final and complete consummation lies in the future and will occur when this age is over and God's kingdom reigns on earth as in heaven. (Argyle, 10–11)

Jesus taught that, in his ministry, the kingdom had already arrived (4:17; 10:7; 12:28; 16:28). The kingdom broke in with the teaching of Christ, but a complete fulfillment still lies in the future. From the reference in 16:28, Jesus indicates that the fulfillment would come in the lifetime of his disciples, and so the early church believed the arrival was imminent.

Jesus' miracles and healings were both a demonstration and an embodiment of the presence of the kingdom. He commissioned his disciples to embody the kingdom's presence as well (10:7–8). Matthew assures his community that the exalted Lord is present in their midst to make the sick well and to give the demon-possessed peace of mind and spirit. To identify with Christ and become his disciple means to enter the kingdom and receive eternal life, which is everlasting, full, and abundant, like life in the blessed messianic age (19:16–30) (Luz, 67).

Before his disciples embody the kingdom, the Lord paves their way in a confrontation with the adversary. We have a lot at stake in the standoff between Jesus and Satan: our future depends on the strength of one will against another. Our Savior goes up against our seducer; our advocate faces our adversary; our transformer goes head-to-head with our tempter. The outcome is crucial not only to Jesus' identity, but to ours.

> "We encounter the 'true God' in the one who rejected the superhuman temptation to 'be like God.' " —Eduard Schweizer, *The Good News according to Matthew*, 65.

Few contemporary readers have been sashayed around by Satan, taunted to turn stones into bread, to jump from steeples, or to lay our souls in Satan's hands. What do our temptations have to do with those uttered to Jesus by the seductive lips of Satan?

All three temptations have as a common denominator the subtle suggestion to treat God as less than God. The first temptation is the enticement to rely on self instead of God's promise to provide. Jesus is participating in a voluntary fast, a spiritual discipline where one abstains from food in order to nourish oneself wholly upon God's will and word. In the Bible, fasting is often a preparation for a great spiritual struggle. In Deuteronomy 9:9, Moses fasted forty days and nights in preparation for receiving the Ten Commandments on Mount Sinai.

Jesus is near the end of his forty-day fast, and his physical desire to break the vow of fasting sets the stage for the first temptation. Satan tests Jesus' full obedience to and reliance upon God; Satan tempts Jesus to rely on his own power for the gratification of his physical needs. The response of Jesus shows that Satan has misunderstood the situation. Jesus' needs are not only physical but also spiritual. Jesus harks back to the story from the Hebrew Scriptures, where God feeds manna to the doubt-ridden children of Israel. Drawing on Deuteronomy 8:3, Jesus affirms that the word of God is more vital to human existence than food. As God took care of the faithful of old, so also would God care for him in the absence of familiar food.

Another dimension to the first temptation is an attempt by Satan to play into what he hopes will be Jesus' craving for recognition and popular approval. Sometimes the Romans distributed free bread to gain the people's favor. The Jews of the first century saw material abundance as a sign of the Messiah's arrival. To turn stones into bread is also a temptation for Jesus to fulfill the people's messianic expectations through a sleight of hand.

The second temptation is the enticement to rely on God, but to negotiate the terms with God. Satan challenges Jesus to test God's care for him in a dramatic, public demonstration. Satan quotes Psalm 91:11–12, understood as a reference to the Messiah. Jesus replies by quoting Deuteronomy 6:16, a reference to the thirsty Israelites testing God at Massah (Ex. 17:1–7). Testing God's good faith betrays our lack of faith. How often do

> "If the evil one cannot make us . . . super-secular by seeking wonder bread, perhaps he can make us superspiritual by suggesting leaps of faith." —Frederick Dale Bruner, *Matthew*, vol. 1, p. 108.

we say to God, "Do this one thing for me, and then I'll know that you love me." "Make this problem go away, and then I'll believe in you." "Promise me there will be no downside, no pain involved, and then I'll take this risk." Or, on the flip side, how often, when things go wrong, do we allow appearances to blot out God's promises? How often do we throw faith out the window? By standing up to this second temptation, Jesus shows that the best response to doubt and adversity is to ask for faith instead of outward signs of divine favor.

The third temptation is the enticement to be God. Satan offers Jesus the world if he will worship him—no obstacles, no suffering, no pain and a world of gain. Satan saves the most tantalizing temptation until last. If he can get Jesus to succumb to this third temptation, he can work backward and get Jesus to yield to the first two. Satan will be signed on as Jesus' public relations manager in no time flat! But seeing what he stands to gain by making bread out of stones and leaping from steeples only reminds Jesus of what he would stand to lose. Later, in Matthew 16:26 he warns his disciples: "What will it profit them if they gain the whole world but forfeit their life? Or what will they give in return for their life?"(16:26).

Thus Jesus demonstrates that the Son of God lives by a bold obedience to God that takes the form of an active righteousness in the face of powerful temptations. Jesus declines the third temptation, so for Satan, for the moment anyway, it's three strikes and he is out. Earlier Jesus refused to call for angels for the wrong reasons, so now they come unsummoned when he needs their nourishment most. "Then the devil left him, and suddenly angels came and waited on him" (4:11). Jesus refused to manipulate God, and then is nourished by God.

Satan

There are Christians who give a great deal of attention to the biblical figure of the devil, understanding him as a literal, personal force in the world. They make him responsible for the injustice, moral failure, and cruelty that is embodied by individuals and groups. Some see him as a scapegoat for both their failings and society's failings. Satanists see him as an object of worship. In the preface to his satirical look at temptation, *The Screwtape Letters,* C. S. Lewis makes this comment: "There are two equal and opposite errors into which our race can fall about the devils. One is to disbelieve in their existence. The other is to believe and to feel an excessive and unhealthy interest in them" (Lewis, 9).

In the pages of scripture, Satan is a metaphor for evil, or in literary terms, a personification that draws into one mythical being all the images and concepts theorized about evil by the Israelites throughout their history. He represents the existence of evil both in people and the world. His role should be taken seriously because something is radically wrong with the perspectives and actions of people. Like lava, corruption bubbles up from the depths of people's inward lives, and, finally, spills over the boundaries of their private lives to solidify into unjust systems. This corruption is so deeply imbedded and tortuously intertwined in human existence that only God's power in Christ can dig it out or unravel the tangled skein.

Being naïve about evil can lead to an unprotected openness to superficial self-help religion or the influence of persuasive but misguided leaders. At the same time, to take evil seriously means to take responsibility for the embodiment of evil in individuals and shared communities.

Jesus was tempted by enticements that tempted those in Matthew's day, and do so now in ours. Part of the forbidden thrill of temptation is the moment of wavering. In that moment, the half-hearted want to give in to the temptation. As someone wryly said, "I can resist anything except temptation." Jesus modeled for all believers how to combat temptation. Like Jesus, those tempted can draw on scripture to overcome the enticement that lies before them. Like Jesus, remembering God's providential care in times past can give believers the vision to battle temptation. Like Jesus, recognizing what can be lost in the face of what can be gained can help banish the adversary.

Want to Know More?

About Satan? See Shirley C. Guthrie, *Christian Doctrine*, rev. ed. (Louisville, Ky.: Westminster John Knox Press, 1994), 166–91, esp. 179–82.

About Jesus' baptism? For a thorough, but technical, discussion on the reasons for Jesus' baptism, see George R. Beasley-Murray, *Baptism in the New Testament* (Grand Rapids: Wm. B. Eerdmans Publishing Co., 1973), 45–67.

About different understandings of baptism? See Alan Richardson and John Bowden, *The Westminster Dictionary of Christian Theology* (Philadelphia: Westminster Press, 1983), 299–302; J. G. Davies, ed., *The Westminster Dictionary of Liturgy and Worship* (Philadelphia: Westminster Press, 1986), 55–77; Ted A. Campbell, *Christian Confessions: A Historical Introduction* (Louisville, Ky.: Westminster John Knox Press, 1996).

About fasting? See Marjorie J. Thompson, *Soul Feast: An Invitation to the Christian Spiritual Life* (Louisville, Ky.: Westminster John Knox Press, 1995), 69–81.

Questions for Reflection

1. It is said that Martin Luther would remind himself of his identity as a Christian by saying to himself, "I am baptized. I am baptized." How does being baptized change a person's identity?

2. If Satan placed three temptations before us today, what would they be? Where are we spiritually vulnerable? When are we tempted to protect our own self-interests?

3. There is a tension in this passage in the portrayal of the Spirit— present in the parting of the clouds at Jesus' baptism, but leading

Jesus to a trial by fire into the wilderness. What does this suggest about the function of the Spirit in the life of the believer?

4. Many see a connection between the presentation of the life of Moses in Exodus and the life of Jesus in Matthew. What are some of the similarities between the lives of these two? What are some of the differences?

The Sermon on the Mount: Part One

While Jesus is being tempted in the desert, John the Baptist is being arrested by Herod. The incarceration of John becomes a turning point in Jesus' ministry. He withdraws to Galilee and begins, like John, to preach a message of repentance. In the verses that lead up to the Sermon on the Mount (4:12–25), the evangelist emphasizes two key points. First, the Messiah's ministry will fulfill scripture by bringing light to those in darkness (4:12–17). Matthew sees Jesus' ministry as a fulfillment of the prophet Isaiah, again using a quotation from the Suffering Servant poems (Isa. 42:7). The first words of Jesus' public ministry echo John's first words, "Repent, for the kingdom of heaven has come near" (4:17). His next words, "Follow me, and I will make you fish for people" (4:19), compel his first disciples to leave their nets without a backward look and join his ministry.

[margin note: 1ST WORDS]

[margin note: TEACHING PREACHING]

Second, the Messiah's healing ministry, important as it is, is in the service of his teaching and preaching ministry (4:23–25). His ministry of teaching, preaching, and healing attracts great crowds that cluster around the mountain. Matthew presents Jesus, like Moses, as going up on a mountain to give the authoritative revelation to the people from God. The Messiah is a teacher par excellence. Through his teaching he will bring light to the nations.

"When Jesus saw the crowds, he went up the mountain."

Righteousness [handwritten in left margin]

The Basic Themes of the Sermon

A continuing theme of Matthew's Gospel is that of genuine righteousness, a righteousness that purifies the inward life and energizes the faithful to seek justice for the vulnerable. This theme is described in detail in the Sermon on the Mount, where Jesus exhorts his hearers to be obedient to the law of God and to exceed the zeal for righteousness of even the Pharisees (5:17–20). The Sermon on the Mount is the first and longest of five collections of Jesus' teachings in Matthew (chaps. 5–7; 10; 13; 18; 24–25). The Sermon paints Jesus as Israel's ultimate, God-authorized teacher. The message for readers is clear: believing in Jesus means living in accordance with his teachings.

Even though the Sermon contains a number of warnings (see, e.g., 7:21–27), the main focus calls for joyful, light-bearing obedience to Christ. Followers of Jesus are to live this new righteousness themselves and to teach it to others. The Great Commission at the end of the Gospel (28:18–20) commands the apostles not to enlist the nations merely as believers, but as *obedient* disciples. The apostles are to teach people "to obey everything that I have commanded you," and the Sermon on the Mount is the heart of these commandments that they are to teach the Gentiles (Luz, 43).

How many beatitudes were there?

Matthew (in 3d person)	Luke (in 2d person)
5:3 the poor	6:20 you who are poor
5:4 they who mourn	6:21 you who weep
5:5 the meek	
5:6 the hungry	6:21 you who are hungry
5:7 the merciful	
5:8 the pure in heart	
5:9 the peacemakers	
5:10 the persecuted	
5:11 you who are reviled	6:22 you who are hated
	6:24 woe to you who are rich
	6:25 woe to you who are fed
	6:25 woe to you who laugh
	6:26 woe to you who are spoken well of

The Sermon is found in both Matthew and Luke (indeed, many scholars believe that Matthew and Luke were each using a common collection of the sayings of Jesus, a document now lost to us but one to which scholars refer as "Q"). Even though both Matthew and Luke include the Sermon, there are differences. For example, there is a difference in geography. In Matthew, Jesus delivers the Sermon on a mountain (5:1). Luke's account could be more accurately named "The Sermon on the Plain," because Jesus delivers the Sermon while standing "on a level place" (Luke 6:17). There is also a difference in audience. In Luke, the Sermon is addressed primarily to the outcasts of society, to the poor and to those on the receiving end of oppressive relationships and institutions. Matthew's Sermon is addressed to all who need God, regardless of their economic condition. Luke's version of the Sermon includes woes upon the rich (Luke 6:24–26), but these are conspicuously absent in Matthew.

Also, there is a difference in theological emphasis. In Luke, the Sermon follows a series of healing stories (see Luke 5–6), and the spotlight falls on the role of Jesus as healer (see especially Luke 6:17–19). By contrast, although Matthew does state that Jesus has performed many healings, the Sermon on the Mount is the first act of Jesus' public ministry that Matthew describes in detail. This first act serves to emphasize the primacy of teaching in his overall ministry.

What does Jesus teach in the Sermon on the Mount? He teaches his followers that they are "the salt of the earth" (5:13) and "the light of the world" (5:14), and he calls them to "be perfect" as their heavenly Father is perfect (5:48). But can human beings be perfect? Can human beings measure up to the new righteousness like that proclaimed in the Sermon on the Mount? Throughout history, interpreters have struggled with the apparent double bind of the Sermon: on the one hand, Jesus makes seemingly impossible ethical demands and, on the other, warns about judgment for those who cannot keep them.

A closer look at the Sermon, however, leads us to see the Sermon not as an impossible demand, not as a threat, but as a gift from God. First, the setting on the mountain calls to mind the giving of the law on Mount Sinai (Ex. 19:16–25). The faithful God who led the Israelites through the Red Sea and gave the law, regarded by Jews as God's greatest gift to them, is the same God who now leads the people in the form of Jesus (Luz, 48). This new law is not a burden, but a life-giving treasure lavished upon the people

31

by God. Matthew wants his readers to view the Sermon on the Mount as a definitive interpretation of the Torah (the first five books of the Hebrew Scriptures), the nucleus of which Moses received on Mount Sinai. Jesus does not cancel the Mosaic law by substituting a new legal code. Instead, Jesus fulfills Torah by providing the proper interpretation.

Another indication that the Sermon is not an impossible catalog of demands is the key place given to prayer. In the middle of the Sermon is the Lord's Prayer. God is depicted in the Sermon as one who does not leave human beings to rise or fall on our own efforts, but who responds to human need expressed through prayer. The command to righteousness that exceeds that of the scribes and Pharisees (5:20) is enabled by the Father who knows and hears the pleas of those who will ask, seek, and knock (7:7–11).

The Setting of the Sermon

The Sermon begins when Jesus sees the crowds and goes up onto a mountain. The setting of a mountain significant. Not only does it call to mind Sinai; the mountain also represents a place where Jesus and his disciples go for prayer, vision, and empowerment (14:23; 15:29; 17:1; 28:16). Separated from the regular routine of their lives, the disciples are on the mountain, a place of holiness and an ideal location to form the structure of a new community (Williams, 173).

"He sits like a king on his throne, his disciples approach him like subjects in a royal court, and the king delivers his inaugural address, in which he lays out in considerable detail what life in his kingdom will be like." Douglas R. A. Hare, *Matthew*, Interpretation, 35.

After Jesus went up the mountain, he sat down. Although this little detail might seem trivial, it actually has considerable importance. To sit down to teach communicates the customary posture of a Jewish teacher, that of a scribe or rabbi. In this teaching then, Jesus is portrayed as presenting an authoritative scribal teaching (Williams, 173). The Sermon is addressed first to the disciples, who then will spread the good news to others through their missionary preaching. Though not the immediate audience, the crowd is also addressed, for they "were astounded at his teaching, for he taught them as one having authority, and not as their scribes" (7:28).

32

The Beatitudes

Beatitudes are common in the Old Testament (see Isa. 30:18; Jer. 17:7). Beatitudes are also found in Greek literature where the blessings promised are largely materialistic (Argyle, 44). Scholars have debated whether the Beatitudes are commands that must be obeyed to enter the kingdom of God or statements of the blessings available to those who trust in God. Rather than being either commands or blessings, the Beatitudes might be a combination of the two. Instead of being entry requirements for God's acceptance, the Beatitudes describe the joyful response God enables in those who actively accept God. Each beatitude combines elements of both promise and challenge, for us today as well as for the original readers.

The word "blessed" begins each beatitude. The literal translation is "Oh, the blessedness of . . ." In the biblical context, blessedness describes happiness that comes from a right relationship with God, as opposed to a more material understanding of good fortune or emotional bliss. Psalm 1:1–2 states: "Happy are those who do not follow the advice of the wicked . . . but their delight is in the law of the LORD, and on his law they meditate day and night." And again Psalm 33:12 offers: "Happy is the nation whose God is the LORD, the people whom he has chosen as his heritage."

God is the unexpressed subject of the action in the second part of many beatitudes. "Blessed are those who . . . , for God will comfort, fill, and give mercy."

> **How do different translations render "blessed"?**
>
> *Today's English Version:* "Happy"
> *Cotton Patch:* "They are God's people"
> *William Barclay:* "O the bliss of those"
> *Robert Funk:* "Congratulations"

Blessedness does not call for a state of passive resignation to present hardships. Rather, God gives blessedness to those who remain faithful despite present adversities. Blessedness causes new orientations of thought and action, along with a subsequent newness in states of life. The Beatitudes express the newness that God makes possible in the life and activity of Jesus (Hill, 110).

Matthew's version of the Beatitudes, in contrast to Luke's, emphasizes the inward disposition of a person, rather than the nature of one's outward circumstances. Whereas Luke's beatitude may speak to one who is outwardly poor, Matthew's version speaks to the inwardly poor. In Luke, the audience is those who are physically hungry. In Matthew, the hungry are seekers of righteousness.

Blessedness has a sense of immediacy, a sense of this world, of now. Blessedness is discovered in the midst of Christ's restoration of this creation and this life. Although beginning and growing in this present life, blessedness will be fully realized only in the time to come (Hill, 110).

The Poor in Spirit (5:3)

The New English Bible translation of this verse captures best the intention: "How blest are these who know their need of God." In contrast to Luke, Matthew apparently believed that equating riches with sin was an oversimplification, just as was equating poverty with piety. Israel knew firsthand that the dangers of prosperity too often led to forgetfulness of God (Deut. 8:11–18). Israel's wisdom tradition knew that both riches and poverty could lead the foolish to turn aside from God (Prov. 30:7–9). Matthew's version doesn't equate poverty with piety, or wealth with sin. The Sermon neither automatically includes or excludes the rich. "Poor in spirit" refers to those who, regardless of their economic or social status, manifest humble dependence on God's grace. This beatitude promises those who remember their need for God and call upon God, that God will make them contributors to the divine reign on earth.

The beatitude challenges those who forget their need for God and begin scaling the slippery heights of ambition or careening down the canyons of their own insecurities. The quality of being "poor in spirit" is the wellspring of active faith. The unspoken testimony of the lives of the patriarchs and matriarchs, judges, kings, priests, disciples, and apostles witnesses to their dependence on God. In forgetting their need for God, the feet of these saints began to slip, whereupon God called them back to poverty of spirit (Psalm 51). A reminder to be poor in spirit is the repeated clarion call of the prophets to the nation (Isa. 66:2; Hab. 2:4). The psalms are a record of individual and national poverty of spirit: "But I am poor and needy; hasten to me, O God!" (Ps. 70:5).

In Jesus' ministry, most often the people who had the least to lose in material terms responded most fully to Jesus (4:24–25). There were also people, among them unnamed women, who, though materially comfortable, discovered their need for God through Jesus' teachings (26:6–13). They opened their homes to him and his disciples, sharing their food and other resources to support his itinerant, not-for-profit ministry (8:14–15).

The people of Israel were well aware that "the fear of the LORD is the beginning of knowledge" (Prov. 1:7). Such fear is not a sweaty-palmed foreboding of God's intent to harm. Rather, the fear of the Lord acknowledges that God is the ultimate source of insight and wisdom. Proper fear of God is much akin to being poor in spirit.

> "The Beatitudes turn the world's values upside down. . . . The people whom the world would see as pitiful . . . are the very people Jesus claims are truly joyful."
> —Thomas G. Long, *Matthew*, Westminster Bible Companion, 47.

The Mournful (5:4)

This beatitude should not be reduced only to an individual level. To be sure, this beatitude is also about the mourning of those who have lost loved ones and the mourning of those whose consciences repent over their past sins, but it is also about a public mourning over the sins of society. The background of this beatitude is Isaiah 61:1–4, where God's Servant is anointed with the Spirit to bring good news to the poor and "to comfort all who mourn; to provide for those who mourn in Zion—to give them a garland instead of ashes, the oil of gladness instead of mourning, the mantle of praise instead of a faint spirit. . . . They shall build up the ancient ruins." This passage in Isaiah speaks to the period after the exile, when Israel mourned her devastation by the Babylonians, as well as the national moral failure the prophets insisted had caused the exile in the first place.

In Jesus' day, the Romans presided over a system where the people were heavily taxed and poverty was common. Both the Jewish and Roman elite viewed the poor, peasants, prostitutes, and lepers as an expendable commodity. Matthew's word of blessing is upon both those who mourn because of their own state of life and those who mourn because others suffer injustices. Mourning is for the plight of the whole nation, which suffers in subjection and injustice.

This beatitude promises that those who mourn because of economic injustice or personal sorrow have God's ear. The beatitude challenges those who are materially comfortable and possess emotional reserves. In a powerful message to both the church and individuals, they are to act as agents of God's comfort now.

Alexander Gonzales Jr., a youth director at La Trinidad Church in San Antonio, is an agent of God's comfort. In addition to holding a separate full-time job, Gonzales spends more than fifty hours a week with gang members and other teens in his fifty-member youth group. He gains their trust by showing them that he cares and believes in them. Without pressing his friendship, Gonzales talks to them when they are at ease and attends all performances or games in which they participate. His befriending the gang members has led many to leave the gangs, and a number of those youth pursue higher education after high school. To leave a gang, though, some young people must go through a brutal ritual. Says Gonzales, "I was there for one young man who had to walk the line. He got beat up, kicked, and hit before they let him go" (Peck-Stahl, 25). Gonzales brings God's presence into the lives of these young people as he seeks justice, not only for their physical predicaments, but for their spirits as well.

The Meek (5:5)

Psalm 37:11 supplies the backdrop to this verse: "But the meek shall inherit the land, and delight themselves in abundant prosperity." This psalm may have offered the promise of a more equitably proportioned reward to small landowners. As an added bonus, the wealthy oppressing landowners would control their lives no longer. Matthew probably interpreted Psalm 37 in a spiritual sense; inheriting the land meant entering the new land of God's kingdom. The meek would participate in a new community of obedience and righteousness (Hill, 112).

The Bible gives several examples of meekness. Moses is described as being meek in Numbers 12:3, and Matthew 11:29 and 21:5 describe Jesus this way. Meekness does not connote the quality of being a doormat. Rather, to be meek refers to a humility that comes from being poor in spirit. The humble are those who know they have need of the Great Physician (9:12). In this sense, this beatitude is a commentary on the preceding one.

> "Without humility there can be no true religion, for all true religion begins with a realization of our own weakness and of our need for God." —William Barclay, *The Gospel of Matthew,* Daily Study Bible, vol. 1, p. 97.

People who realize their need for God also realize what they don't need any longer—the need to get the better of others, or to lord possessions or position over others, or to resort to violence. *The Interpreter's Dictionary of the Bible* (ed. Buttrick, 3:334) defines "meekness" as complete dependence on God, and Webster's refers to a long-suffering patience in the face of injury (*Webster's Third New International Dictionary, Unabridged* [1961], 1403). Francis de Sales, a seventeenth-century bishop and spiritual writer, commended the "little virtues" of gentleness, kindness, patience, simplicity, and mutual regard. These virtues were more than just good manners, and chief among them was gentleness, or meekness. The person who could be meek while enduring sorrow or suffering, and at peace while bombarded by the multiplicity and busyness of affairs, was a person whose life reflected the kingdom that Jesus preached (Wright, 39–40).

This beatitude promises that, if we allow God to instill in us this little virtue of meekness and humility, our reward will be great indeed. The beatitude challenges us to believe stubbornly in an unreasonable truth in the face of overwhelming cultural appearances to the contrary. Jesus stubbornly resisted Satan's temptation to take a showy leap off a steeple. To both Moses and Jesus, scripture pays the highest compliment—that they were humble. Perhaps meekness was a key ingredient in their visionary leadership of the people of God. Both the promise and the challenge of this beatitude are that the path of meekness, or humility, is the path by which the last become first and thereby lead whole communities in paths of active obedience to God (Phil. 2:8–11).

> ## Want to Know More?
>
> **About the Sermon on the Mount?** See Robert H. Stein, *The Method and Message of Jesus' Teachings,* rev. ed. (Louisville, Ky.: Westminster John Knox Press, 1994); Rudolf Schnackenburg, *All Things Are Possible to Believers: Reflections on the Lord's Prayer and the Sermon on the Mount* (Louisville, Ky.: Westminster John Knox Press, 1995).
>
> **About Q?** See Archibald M. Hunter, *Introducing the New Testament,* 3d rev. ed. (Philadelphia: Westminster Press, 1972), 28–33; Celia Brewer Marshall, *A Guide through the New Testament* (Louisville, Ky.: Westminster John Knox Press, 1994), 26–28.

Questions for Reflection

1. The Beatitudes are blessings. What are some blessings in your life? The Beatitudes are also challenges. What are some challenges to your faith?
2. To be "poor in Spirit" is to know one's need for God. What do you need from God?
3. Some years ago, there was a television commercial showing a Native American looking out at a litter-strewn highway. As he gazes over what human beings have done to make creation ugly, a

mournful tear runs down his cheek. In our world, where do we hear the cries of mourning? How would you explain the meaning of Jesus' promise "Blessed are those who mourn" to someone who mourns?

4. In the Sermon on the Mount, Jesus says, "Blessed are the meek." Who are the meek in our society?

What are the money changers? gamblers?

The Sermon on the Mount: Part Two

The Beatitudes in the Sermon on the Mount exist as a unit, so any division for the sake of study is artificial. However, a convenient break exists between the third and fourth beatitudes, as the focus moves from more inward changes to more outward changes. The first three beatitudes—poor in spirit, mourning, and meekness— might be understood as more internal in nature, but the next few beatitudes, although starting inside a person, finally take a more outward and active expression.

The Beatitudes (Continued)

In the previous study session, we explored the first three beatitudes. Now let us examine the rest.

The Seekers of Righteousness (5:6)

In comparison with the stark wording in Luke, "Blessed are you who are hungry" (Luke 6:21), Matthew's wording—"Blessed are those who hunger and thirst for righteousness"—seems spiritualized or sentimentalized. However, this beatitude is not limited to a personal or inward application. Matthew is referring to God's saving righteousness as proclaimed by the prophets, God's vindication of the cause of the afflicted (see Isa. 51:1–5; 61:3).

Understood in this way, the beatitude might be paraphrased to say "Blessed are those who yearn for the manifestation of God's saving righteousness," or, as the New English Bible translates this verse:

"How blest are those who hunger and thirst to see right prevail; they shall be satisfied."

Righteousness for Matthew also embraces a response to God's initiative, living in conformity to God's will (5:10, 20). Once again, the theme of active righteousness appears in the Gospel. The longing for this righteousness must show itself in active obedience, not in passive waiting. Fully embracing a life of righteous obedience is a gift from God (Hill, 112). Herein lies the promise of this beatitude—naming this hungering after righteousness in our communal lives as being the work of God.

When we think it's all up to us, our energies soon flag. We like to form task forces, assign tasks, and bring closure. The buzzword in recruitment in many church circles these days is "short-term commitment." Assuring people that they are being asked for limited output is used as a persuasive device. But sooner or later, the light dawns on these would-be disciples that hungering and thirsting after righteousness means the commitment of a lifetime, a commitment that proceeds slowly and experiences frequent setbacks. This beatitude assures that God is on our side, and that our persistence, even in the face of two steps forward with one step backward, is undergirded by grace.

> "This beatitude is in reality a question and a challenge. In effect it demands, 'How much do you want goodness? Do you want it as much as a starving man wants food, and as much as a man dying of thirst wants water?'" —William Barclay, *The Gospel of Matthew*, Daily Study Bible, vol. 1, p. 100.

Perhaps the challenge of this beatitude lies in the very accessibility of righteousness it portrays. God is willing and able to help believers embrace and live the promise. A word of caution, though; this beatitude warns backhandedly that there is no excuse not to avail oneself of this righteousness.

The Merciful (5:7)

For Matthew, mercy is a broad term that embraces both compassion and forgiveness. Typical of Matthew's emphasis on active righteousness, mercy is more an action than an attitude. In Matthew 23:23, the scribes and Pharisees are criticized. They are accused of being attentive to outward rituals and negligent about the heart of the law: justice and mercy and faith.

A surface reading of the beatitude might suggest incorrectly that God's mercy toward us is contingent on our mercy toward others.

But Matthew wants his readers to grasp the gracious initiative of God, which places the motivations for showing mercy in a whole different light. This beatitude encourages gracious charity (almsgiving), motivated by the desire to alleviate suffering rather than to gain prestige (6:2). Mercy is the response to a God who has first shown mercy (18:23–35). The correct motive for showing mercy is loving gratitude toward God and a willingness to be shaped in God's image.

Saint Teresa once dreamed she saw a woman running, carrying a flaming torch in one hand, and a pail of water in the other. When Teresa asked the woman where she was going, she answered, "I am going to quench the fires of hell and burn down the mansions of heaven so that people will love God for God's own sake, not because they fear punishment or seek reward" (Stookey, 36).

Matthew's Gospel forces a confrontation with the reality of the consequences of unresponsiveness and repentance. Participation in God's coming kingdom is promised to those who obey and respond to Jesus. But this is by no means an attempt at a primitive moral scare tactic or bribery. Love and gratitude to God, regardless of reward or punishment, are to be daily motivations. This beatitude promises the continuing reception of mercy and compassion from God, and it challenges us to remember our dependence on those gifts. The beatitude reminds us to lavish those gifts upon the grasping, backbiting, self-centered people with whom we have dealings day to day. Presumably that would include also the person we face in the mirror each morning and evening!

> "The first test of obedience to Jesus' ethic is not whether obedience makes one morally tougher but whether it makes one humanly tenderer—merciful." —Frederick Dale Bruner, *Matthew*, vol. 1, p. 146.

The Pure in Heart (5:8)

In the New Testament, the Greek adjective *katharos* (here translated "pure") connotes both the idea of cleanliness (27:59 refers to a clean linen shroud) and the idea of purity, in the sense of unalloyed, as in the pure gold of Revelation 21:21. The Old Testament background to this verse is probably Psalm 24:4–5: "Those who have clean hands and pure hearts, who do not lift up their souls to what is false, and do not swear deceitfully. They will receive blessing from the LORD, and vindication

> Do clean hands make a pure heart? Was Pilate's washing of his hands (27:24) an attempt to clean his heart?

from the God of their salvation." These are those who are spiritually pure rather than ritually or ceremonially clean.

In Matthew's beatitude, a combination of clean and pure is probably intended. Because the heart in Hebrew thought was the seat of the will, the beatitude may be intending the sense "Blessed are those who are innocent of moral failures (deeds) and of evil intentions." Again, Matthew's beatitudes emphasize the inward disposition of a person that leads to changed behavior. Jesus describes the heart as the wellspring of evil intentions that become evil deeds (15:19). He speaks of those who honor God in words while their hearts are far removed from God (15:8).

Purity of heart cannot be achieved without God's help. Arrogance, self-centeredness, and hard-hearted, unforgiving attitudes toward others poison the heart. These poisons create a state that stands in contrast to the blessed states described in the beatitudes that preceded this one. The pure in heart are those who consistently and repeatedly allow God to cleanse them of corruption. Their devotion is single-minded. They do not attempt to serve both mammon and God (6:24). Their life's wellspring, their heart, is pure. They are like trees that, out of their goodness, bear good fruit (12:33–37).

To "see God" is a metaphor for the bliss of fellowship with and knowledge of God in the kingdom to come (Ps. 17:15; 1 Cor. 13:12). Seeing God face-to-face is a theme that plays throughout the Old Testament. The people are told through prophets to seek God's face (Hos. 5:15). The psalmists long for a vision of God's face as a positive blessing and almost chide God at times for its elusiveness (Pss. 44:24; 102:2). At the same time, danger is implied when imperfect humans come face-to-face with God (Gen. 32:30; Isa. 6:5). Indeed, says God, "No one shall see me and live"(Ex. 33:20), except for Moses.

There are two scriptural statements that put Moses in a class by himself. One relates to the intimacy of his experience of God. "Never since has there arisen a prophet in Israel like Moses, whom the LORD knew face to face" (Deut. 34:10). A second relates to his meekness. "Now the man Moses was very humble, more so than anyone else on the face of the earth" (Num. 12:3).

In the New Testament, Jesus reveals God out of his firsthand knowledge as the Son (John 1:18). We are adjured to focus our gaze on the face of Jesus Christ, through whom we will receive the light of the knowledge of the glory of God (2 Cor. 4:6). Maintaining this focus, we are transformed gradually into those who are pure in heart.

The pure in heart are those who recognize their need for God, who empathize with and extend comfort to others, who humble themselves before God and others, and whose lives are graced by daily deeds of compassionate forgiveness to those who wrong them. God offers gifts to help purify the heart and deepen relationship with God through the daily practice of spiritual disciplines, which include searching the scriptures, gathering as the worshiping body of Christ, celebrating the sacraments of Baptism and the Lord's Supper, engaging in unprovoked deeds of charity and both public and private prayer.

The daily discipline of prayer is too often neglected because of busyness with other things or misunderstanding prayer's purpose. Spiritual director James Fenhagen tells of asking a group of people at a prayer retreat to finish the sentence "Prayer is . . ." Most of them chose the phrase "something we ought to do." That, says Fenhagen, is like saying we ought to breathe. Prayer, he insists, is a thirst that is much deeper than "ought" (Fenhagen, 28–29). Prayer helps individuals enter the blessed state the Beatitudes hold out as both gifts and challenges. Prayer casts out anxiety and envy, and makes room for singleness of purpose amid the distractions of daily life. Prayer is the path to the peace that passeth understanding; it is a daily nourishment for the rigorous task of peacemaking in a hostile world.

The Peacemakers (5:9)

Peacemakers are not only those who live in peace, practicing nonresistance, but those who work for peace, who commit their efforts to the uphill task of bringing harmony between warring individuals, communities, and even countries. Peacemakers are those who work to bring about peace, overcoming evil with good. The Hebrew word *shalom* (peace) denotes not just the absence of conflict but the presence of loving harmony and justice within communities. The Roman legions who had established the Pax Romana (the peace of Rome) could end military conflict, but could not establish *shalom*.

> Glen Stassen suggests that peacemaking is not a *protest against something* but is instead a *transforming initiative* to break the underlying bondage that often erupts into violence. See Glen H. Stassen, *Just Peacemaking: Transforming Initiatives for Justice and Peace* (Louisville, Ky.: Westminster John Knox Press, 1992), p. 42 and throughout the book.

A major wall exists in today's churches between middle-class congregations and the poor, or as theologian and seminary professor Tex

Sample says, "between hard living people and mainstream Christians." He draws a distinction between charity and true servanthood. There are plenty of ministries *to* hard living people, but fewer ministries *with* them. The poor are seen as down-and-outers, not brothers or sisters in Christ. Sample challenges churches to be peacemakers and to break down the wall (Eph. 2:14). Churches should move past charity to mutual ministry (Sample, *Hard Living People and Mainstream Christians*).

This kind of peacemaking, this breaking down of traditional barriers between people, is far riskier than that of writing checks or collecting canned goods, important as those charitable activities are. There is the risk that values might be challenged and relationships might be forged between groups that have nothing in common but the love of Christ and commitment to being his body on earth. There is the risk that they may contribute to God's presence becoming real on earth. Near the beginning of Matthew, an angel whispers the key to Jesus' identity into the ear of his sleeping father-to-be: "They shall name him Emmanuel, which means, God is with us." Peacemakers have God with them also.

> There cannot be peace without forgiveness. And "whenever forgiveness awes us, or helps us know our place in creation, or connects us to one another, or interprets us to ourselves, we are meeting God." — Maria Harris, *Proclaim Jubilee: A Spirituality for the Twenty-first Century* (Louisville, Ky.: Westminster John Knox Press, 1996), 39.

The activity of peacemaking is emphasized in the rabbinical literature and in the writings of Judaism between the Old and New Testaments: "Blessed is he who brings peace and love" (*2 Enoch* 52:11). Creators of *shalom* live by the proactive righteousness Jesus teaches, even when peace goes against their natural inclinations and ingrained social convention. Peacemakers build bridges while others are constructing walls; they strive to love their enemies and return good for evil. Their efforts are judged, not by secular standards, but by God. God bestows on peacemakers the title "children of God," Israel's destiny and title (Deut. 14:1; Hos. 1:10). The peacemakers are the true Israel.

Those Persecuted for Righteousness (5:10-12)

Righteousness means faithfulness and obedience to the law of God as interpreted by Jesus. Jesus' teachings were radical; to follow them meant to upset social norms. This becomes increasingly clear as the

Sermon continues. To live by the teachings of Jesus meant to embrace voluntary poverty (6:19–21), love of enemies (5:43–48), non-retaliation (5:38–42), a cutting loose of home and family ties (8:22; 10:34–39; 12:46–50), and a fearless and carefree attitude toward life based on confidence in God's care (6:25–34).

This final beatitude grouping reflects the opposition Jewish-Christian missionaries of Matthew's day encountered in their attempts to live by and to spread the good news. Such opposition from outside helped the group cohere and develop an identity. The term for "be glad" in 5:12 is often a technical term for joy in persecution and martyrdom used in the New Testament (1 Peter 1:6, 8; 4:13; Rev. 19:7).

Verse 11 reflects the tradition in Israel that the true prophets from God through the ages had been persecuted and destroyed (2 Chron. 36:15–16; Neh. 9:26; Acts 7:52; Matt. 23:34). In Matthew's view, those Christians who preached the good news to fellow Jews fulfilled the prophetic function. A good reputation in the community was important in the Jewish tradition, and being publicly reviled was dreaded. The evangelist assures Jesus' followers that, whatever their peers may say about them now, God will grant them glory in the kingdom of heaven that is to come.

Many people have never learned to take criticism or to be opposed, and so shrink back from assuming positions of leadership. Popularity, or at least being noncontroversial and inoffensive, is too often considered crucial to the survival of relationships or career. This beatitude grouping promises that God's call is to faithfulness and integrity, not popularity. God will be faithful to those who buck the tide in service of the gospel. People of courage and leadership in the Bible are those who allow the voice of God, rather than the voice of the people, to deter and to direct them. Examples of this courage are Moses, David, Samuel, Elisha, Jeremiah, Vashti, Esther, Joseph, Mary, the disciples of Jesus, and the women, who stand by the cross and spread the postresurrection good news to both Jesus' enemies and his disciples.

Jesus and the Law and the Prophets

The statement of Jesus regarding the Law and the Prophets (5:17–20) is a preface to the section of the Sermon called "the antitheses," teachings that Jesus prefaces with the words "You have heard that it was said, . . . but I say to you" (5:21–48). Clearly, the antitheses present Jesus as the one to whom God had given definitive authority to interpret the law. The preceding verses clarify the relationship between Jesus and the law, and between his followers and the law. A helpful paraphrase of verse 17 would be "Do not suppose that my mission is to abrogate (repeal or do away with) the law or the prophets' interpretation of the law; my mission is not to abrogate, but rather to confirm the law and the prophets by interpreting Scripture in terms of God's ultimate will" (Hare, 47).

Verse 18 shows that Jesus shared the view of first-century Jews that scripture was inspired by God and could not be set aside. Verse 19 is aimed probably at radical believers who rejected the authority of scripture. Disagreements about how to interpret certain passages abounded then as now. Sadduces, Pharisees, Essenes, and others disagreed vociferously about how various passages should be interpreted and applied.

This high view of scripture did not prevent innovative interpretation that departed radically from the strict letter of the law. By Jesus' day, many prescriptions of the Mosaic code had become dead letters, including most of the death penalty rules. Thus Matthew's Jesus can affirm the authority of scripture and that scripture will be fulfilled in God's good kingdom (when "heaven and earth pass away"). He can also affirm that his interpretation is authoritative, in keeping with the ultimate will of God. When the scribes taught, they cited other rabbinical interpretations to give their own credibility. So when Jesus finished his Sermon on the Mount, "the crowds were astounded at his teaching, for he taught them as one having authority, and not as their scribes" (7:28–29).

Faithfulness to his interpretation leads to a righteousness that exceeds that of the scribes and Pharisees, not in quantity but in quality. The Pharisees were concerned to preserve the distinctiveness of Judaism and had numerous interpretations of Torah concerning ritual cleanliness, dietary habits, and Sabbath activities. These were designed to be constant reminders of God's faithfulness in the midst of the details of everyday life. In practice, they could become substitutes for inward obedience.

The authority of the messianic teacher lies in the fulfillment of the law. He comes not to abolish the Law or the Prophets, but to fulfill them. Not a dot or iota of the law will perish until the fulfillment of God's designs. Even the least of the commandments is to be obeyed (5:20). Frank Kermode has called this a "rhetoric of excess"

(Alter and Kermode, 387–401). Not even the smallest mark of the written Torah is to be considered null. Even the least of the commandments is to be observed. The members of the elect community must be more righteous than the acknowledged teachers of the Torah, whose opponents called them "separatists" (Pharisees). The disciples of Jesus are to be even more "separated" than the Pharisees. Their righteousness is to be radical or they will never enter the kingdom (5:20).

Jesus' followers' obedience must be faithful to the spirit of Torah as revealed to them by Jesus. That obedience is manifested in ethical behavior, even when their behavior is at odds with ritual convention (7:12). This obedience is a precursor to the active righteousness, which is thematic to this Gospel. True obedience is the common denominator of Jesus' teachings on adultery, divorce, oaths, retaliation, almsgiving, prayer, and fasting that follow this passage. Obedience is explicitly expressed in Jesus' teachings about trees and their fruits (7:15–20). The theme continues in Jesus' warning that one must be a doer, not just a hearer, to enter into the kingdom of heaven (7:21–28).

Thomas Merton, a Trappist monk who was instrumental in establishing dialogue between Christians and Buddhists, once met the Dalai Lama, the spiritual leader of the Tibetan Buddhists. The Dalai Lama posed this question to Merton: "What do your vows oblige you to do? Do they simply constitute an agreement to stick around for life in the monastery? Or do they imply a commitment to a life of progress up certain mystical stages?"

Unable to answer quickly, Merton eventually said, "I believe my vows can be interpreted as a commitment to a total inner transformation of one sort or another, a commitment to become a completely new man. No matter where one attempts to do this, that remains the essential thing" (Fenhagen, 4–5).

The rabbinical way of citing scripture was "as it is said." Jesus

> ## Want to Know More?
>
> **About righteousness?** See Alan Richardson and John Bowden, *The Westminster Dictionary of Christian Theology* (Philadelphia: Westminster Press, 1983), 507–8.
>
> **About ritual cleanliness or purity?** See Paul J. Achtemeier, ed., *Harper's Bible Dictionary* (San Francisco: Harper & Row, 1985), 843–44.
>
> **About mourning?** See William Barclay, *New Testament Words* (Philadelphia: Westminster Press, 1974), 224–26.
>
> **About the Lord's Prayer?** See Albert Curry Winn, *A Christian Primer: The Prayer, the Creed, the Commandments* (Louisville, Ky.: Westminster John Knox Press, 1990), 19–80; Rudolf Schnackenburg, *All Things Are Possible to Believers: Reflections on the Lord's Prayer and the Sermon on the Mount* (Louisville, Ky.: Westminster John Knox Press, 1995); Robert H. Stein, *The Method and Message of Jesus' Teachings*, rev. ed. (Louisville, Ky.: Westminster John Knox Press, 1994).

pairs this rabbinical formula with "But I say to you" and then adds some antithetical statements about murder, adultery, divorce, swearing, resistance, and love of neighbor. The Pharisees and the rabbis claimed to be in the "tradition of the fathers," which meant they spoke with the authoritative voice of the elders, those sages of the past who painstakingly transmitted the very words from Mount Sinai. In contrast, Jesus is portrayed as the messianic teacher, one with the authority of God's new reign (Williams, 174).

The Lord's Prayer

For Matthew, the Lord's Prayer is the model for private prayer. It is placed in the midst of a series of warnings against hypocritical piety. The opening, "Our Father," may reflect the beginning of several existing synagogue prayers, and in general, Matthew's version of the Lord's Prayer is very Jewish (Hill, 136).

The prayer is divided into two sets of petitions. The first three petitions ask for God's purposes to be established here and now. "Hallowed be your name, your kingdom come, and your will be done" are tied together by Matthew's characteristic emphasis on active obedience to God. To hallow God's name means to honor God and to glorify God in obedience to divine commands. To hallow God's name prepares for the coming of the kingdom. "Your kingdom come" reflects a petitions which formed the end of every synagogue service, that prayed for the speedy establishment of God's kingdom. For Christians, this kingdom has been inaugurated in the coming of Jesus but is not yet fully realized. "Your will be done" is a petition that reflects Matthew's concern that God's will be obeyed on earth. When God's will is obeyed, the kingdom becomes real (Hill, 136–37).

> **Your kingdom come . . .**
>
> "Does anyone have the foggiest idea what sort of power we so blithely invoke? Or . . . does no one believe a word of it? . . . We should all be wearing crash helmets. Ushers should issue life preservers and signal flares; they should lash us to our pews. For . . . God may draw us out to where we can never return." —Annie Dillard, *Teaching a Stone to Talk: Expeditions and Encounters* (New York: Harper & Row, 1982), 40–41.

The second three petitions are for gifts that the faithful need to live as people of the kingdom. The petition for daily bread recognizes that each day's food for the journey and everyday strength depend upon the constant care of God. The prayer for forgiveness acknowledges our repeated pattern of failure, our constant debt to God, and the need for renewed forgiveness, a forgiveness that is reflected in the forgiveness offered to those who have sinned against us. To pray for deliverance from temptation asks God to protect the followers of Jesus from those places in the path where snares have been set and where the followers may be led astray.

> These petitions in the Lord's Prayer remind us of Jesus' temptations for bread and deliverance.

The Lord's Prayer remains a model for both private prayer and corporate prayer. The priority of God's sovereign will and the straightforward request for divine grace to be obedient make the prayer theologically balanced. Like the Beatitudes, there is a sense of promise and challenge in the Lord's Prayer too. The prayer contains both spiritual nourishment that leaves us satisfied and spiritual urgency that goads us toward God's "already, but not yet" kingdom.

 ## Questions for Reflection

1. Advertisements tell us that we are hungry and thirsty for many things. How do we combat our appetites for material goods or pleasures? What are ways we can encourage the hunger and thirst for righteousness?
2. Mercy or forgiveness can be difficult to give. How does this beatitude speak to issues of crime and punishment?
3. In the discussion of the pure in heart, the term "unalloyed" was used. What does that term mean? What are the things to which we find ourselves alloyed? Certainly we should have commitments to our relationships or to our places of responsibility. How does one balance those commitments with this beatitude?
4. An understanding of the Beatitudes is that they describe the characteristics of God's kingdom. What are those characteristics? The Lord's Prayer pleas for God's kingdom to be here on earth. What are ways that God's kingdom can be evident on earth?

5 Matthew 8:18–27; 15:21–28

Would-Be Disciples and a Lesson about Discipleship

Matthew presents Jesus as a Messiah in deed as well as in word, a model for his disciples. In the Sermon on the Mount, Matthew presented Jesus as the Messiah in word, as a teacher who proclaims the true meaning of God's law. Now Matthew moves to the presentation of Jesus as the Messiah in deed, as a healer and as one who exercises authority over the forces of nature. In chapter 8, Jesus heals a leper, a centurion's servant, and a group of people at Peter's house. He also calms a raging storm at sea, and he challenges would-be disciples with the true cost of following him and putting the kingdom into action in their lives.

Costly Discipleship

Leading up to the narrative of Jesus' stilling of the storm are two brief interchanges between Jesus and potential followers. The first, a scribe, is warned of the rootlessness of following Jesus (8:18–20). Jesus refers to himself, for the first time in Matthew's Gospel, by the mysterious title Son of Man. This title appears also in Mark and Luke. In all three Gospels, the title is always heard on the lips of Jesus himself. No one else ever calls him by this title. Indeed, Son of Man seems to be the only title Jesus chose to use of himself.

The primary background of this title is from the book of Daniel, where "one like unto a son of man" comes with the clouds of heaven unto the Ancient of Days. In Daniel's postexilic context, this figure represents the righteous remnant of Israel, who are brought to glory and vindicated through suffering, as saints of the Most High. Jesus probably used the term to describe his own ministry; he saw himself as a representative of the righteous remnant of Israel whose suffering will be vindicated and used for good by God. In his discussion with the scribe (8:20), Jesus paints the picture of the Son of Man and a loyal community who will experience "a humble, homeless, insecure lot" (Hill, 164).

> "Foxes have holes, and birds of the air have nests; but the Son of Man has nowhere to lay his head." —Matthew 8:20

Another would-be disciple comes to Jesus asking for time to bury his father (8:21–22). Seeing to the burial of a parent was one of the foremost duties of a Jew, one that had a higher priority than many other obligations laid out in the law of Moses. The disciple assumes that he must wait until this obligation has been fulfilled to begin his discipleship. If the father has just died, the delay will be only a short one. Jesus' response seems harsh. However, in keeping with his sayings elsewhere about putting allegiance to God's kingdom first, Jesus asks for priority over even the closest of human relationships (10:37–39; 12:46–50).

These days, family values are held up as virtues and are often used as political platforms. Social critics attribute a variety of problems— gun violence, teen pregnancy, drug use, the rising prison population—to the breakdown of family commitment and communication. On the surface, Jesus' sayings seem to aid the disintegration of families. But on closer look, Jesus demands a loyalty to him that benefits the larger human family. Radical obedience to the divine love for both the righteous and unrighteous (5:43–48) won't allow obligations to one's biological family to override responsibilities to any of God's children. The recognition of the larger human family is expressed eloquently by activist Marian Wright Edelman, founder of the Children's Defense Fund. In her book *The Measure of Our Success: A Letter to My Children and Yours,* she addresses her own three sons and invites the rest of us to listen in. "As a parent I believe that protecting you—my own children—does not end in our kitchen or at our front door or with narrow attention just to your personal needs. . . . As a parent I wanted to make sure you had all your physical needs met and a lot of love. But as a parent I could not ignore other people's children or pain that spills over to public space and threatens the safety and quality of life and pocketbook and future of every American" (30–31).

On an emotional level, discipleship is no painless matter. The disciple is called to a risky life that often will be misunderstood and criticized for making Christ the first priority. Perhaps the criticism may come even from family members. A voyage over choppy seas provides an apt metaphor for the disciple's risky life.

The Storm at Sea

In this story (8:23–27), Jesus calms a powerful storm at sea that threatened to swamp the boat in which he and his disciples were traveling. Some of the church fathers understood the boat in this passage as an image of the church, threatened by persecution and

poverty. The only way to survive amid the pounding waves was by calling on Jesus: "Lord, save us! We are perishing!" (8:25). In the time that the Gospel was written, Jewish-Christian missionaries were vulnerable as they ventured into hostile environments. In those settings, threats and rejection were almost certain. To be faithful to the call of their risen Lord

meant to risk setting sail on uncertain seas. To his credit, Jesus pulled no punches about the high price they would pay.

An anonymous sage has said, "If you don't want to be criticized, don't say anything, do anything, or be anything." Jesus warned that criticism and rejection were inevitable, yet at the same time, he promised his presence at the helm of their ship. The promise is implied in the name God gave him: Emmanuel, God is with us (1:23).

"Lord, save us" is the equivalent of the word *hosanna*, evoking echoes of Psalm 118 and Palm Sunday (Matt. 21:9).

The disciples' cry "Lord, save us!" is a cry that mingles faith with doubt. The disciples doubt that the Lord is attending to their situation. In a submerging boat with a sleeping Savior, he doesn't seem to be. Their cry echoes the demands for help that punctuate the Psalter, or Jesus' last words from the cross, "My God, my God, why have you forsaken me?" (27:46). But their cry is not only about doubt. There is certainty as well. There is faith that Jesus cares about their plight, and that he is their salvation from the difficult situations they face. Theirs is the cry of the poor in spirit, of those who know their need of God.

One commentator helpfully points out that Jesus' miracle stories "transcend past events in the story of Jesus and enter one's own life, encouraging personal experiences with Jesus or making such experiences intelligible" (Luz, 67). This insight rings true in the story of Jesus' stilling the storm. Many people have cried a cry similar to that of the panicking disciples. Some may have experienced violence at the hands of others, situations in which their cry was not met by a rescue rope dropped down from heaven. Surely many of the apostles and martyrs of the church cried a cry like this when faced with danger. Their sailing was seldom smooth. A misreading of the text can conclude that Jesus will smooth out all our choppy seas in the blink of an eye, that he waits at our beck and call to do so. Our experiences cannot support this conclusion.

But perhaps the text advocates an inward state of peaceful confidence in the Lordship of Christ, even in the most chaotic of conditions. Perhaps it advocates the inward state whereby the storms of life are confronted head-on, rather than promising that every storm will be quelled at the outset. We are encouraged to meet any and every storm that besets our lifeboats with faith in Jesus Christ's presence and ultimate victory over the forces of chaos.

Jesus' response in the story yields further insight. In response to the disciples' cry of distress, Jesus uses a word, a favorite in Matthew's Gospel that needs an entire English phrase to do it justice: "you of little faith" (8:26). This phrase refers to those who set out with Jesus but lose heart along the way. Little faith is not a total lack of faith but the presence of an underdeveloped faith, a faith not yet focused and sturdy enough to withstand the challenges of life. Little faith is a faith in process, and perhaps was the type of faith that was prevalent in Matthew's community. Little faith needs to work harder at remembering the promise of God, who is present even in circumstances that seem to indicate divine absence. Still, little faith *is* a faith. As such, perhaps Jesus' words were meant, not as a condemnation, but as encouragement to press on in the faith.

When John Wesley was crossing the Atlantic to serve as a missionary in Georgia, his ship encountered a terrific storm. The gales blew, the ship tilted. Waves soaked his cloak. He clung to a mast to keep from being flung into the sea. He trembled and feared for his life. At the same time, he felt ashamed that he, an ordained cleric, an Oxford don, on a mission to bring the faith to the Indians of South Carolina, should be so filled with fear in the face of death. Looking across the deck, he saw a group of Moravian Christians, among them many children, singing hymns of faith and praise to God.

In his journal for Friday, January 23, 1736, he wrote: "A terrible screaming began among the English. The Germans calmly sang on. I asked one of them afterward, 'Were you not afraid?' He answered, 'I thank God, no.' I asked, 'But were not your women and children afraid?' He replied, mildly, 'No; our women and children are not afraid to die.' " In that moment, John Wesley realized that up until then, his had been a dry-land, fair-weather faith. In his panic, Wesley only focused on his current danger and the imminence of death. He lost sight of God's promises and the centrality of Christ in the life of faith (Wesley, 35).

> "Whether we live or whether we die, we are the Lord's." —Romans 14:8

This Gospel story calls for a revolution in how we view our current situation as individuals and as faith communities. In the fourth century, the astronomer Ptolemy theorized that the earth was the center of the universe, a theory that was accepted without question for several centuries. In the late 1400s, Copernicus realized that the sun was actually the center of the universe, a theory then so radical that he waited until he was on his deathbed to make his ideas public.

After his death, his discovery came to be called the Copernican revolution. Copernicus provides a good analogy for the spiritual revolution we need in our own lives of faith. The disciples in the boat viewed the storm as the center of the situation. In reality, Jesus was the center. This text calls to mind another story of discipleship, the account in Matthew 14:22–33 of Peter walking on the water to Jesus. In both cases, Jesus is the presence of God, Emmanuel, to the disciples. In both cases, maintaining focus on the promises of God's presence in Jesus allows for safe passage through the conflicts.

Matthew began the Gospel by recounting the genealogy, or genesis, of Jesus the Messiah, the son of David, the son of Abraham. In the first Genesis, God's spirit hovered over the chaos, bringing order, light, and a good creation. In this second one, in Jesus' advent, God inaugurates a new creation. In the Sermon on the Mount, Jesus assumes the role "Teacher." With his authority over the storm, Jesus is recognized as Lord, God with us, through whom the chaos of personal and corporate lives can be weathered and even, to a degree, ordered for God's good purposes. Through this powerful narrative, Matthew continues the purpose of his Gospel. He reveals still more about who Jesus is and, in response to him, who we can and ought to be.

The Authority of Jesus

In chapters 9–15, Jesus continues to manifest his authority. He exorcises a demon, an agent of his old nemesis Satan (9:32–34). He heals a paralytic (9:2–8), a hemorrhaging woman (9:22), and two blind men (9:27–31). He resuscitates a dying girl (9:25). He walks on water and empowers a disciple to do likewise (14:22–31). He feeds five thousand people, thus teaching the disciples the source of nourishment they are to share with the spiritually and physically hungry (14:13–21).

Jesus authenticates his authority in his challenge of the traditional interpretation of fasting (9:14–17), Sabbath observance (12:1–14), and the understanding of defilement (15:10–20). Jesus displays authority in his preaching. In a series of parables, he centers on the small, unobtrusive presence of the kingdom of God and employs images like a mustard seed and leaven (13:31–33). He prepares his followers for a coming judgment and cautions them to be wheat, not weeds (13:24–30).

Jesus focuses on the function his authority fulfills and not on the exalted status some want to confer upon him. When the disciples of John the Baptist question the Messiah's identity, Jesus points to the impact of his healings and preaching on the lives of people (11:2–6). He sends forth his followers to perform similar functions of preaching, healing, and exorcising (10:5–15). They are sent only to the Jews (v. 6), but their territory will be expanded in due time.

> ### 📖 Want to Know More?
>
> **About discipleship?** See Shirley C. Guthrie, *Christian Doctrine*, rev. ed. (Louisville Ky.: Westminster John Knox Press, 1994), 330–48.
>
> **About the Son of Man?** See Robert H. Stein, *The Method and Message of Jesus' Teaching*, rev. ed. (Louisville Ky.: Westminster John Knox Press, 1994), 135–51.
>
> **About women in the world of Jesus?** See (if available) Evelyn and Frank Stagg, *Woman in the World of Jesus* (Philadelphia: Westminster Press, 1978); Carol A. Newsom and Sharon H. Ringe, eds. *Women's Bible Commentary*: expand ed. (Louisville Ky.: Westminster John Knox Press, 1998), 482–88.

All of these events happen in the gathering cloud of future persecution, both for Jesus and for those who would share his message. The prediction of persecution probably reflects the experience of missionaries of Matthew's day, when they went forth in the Lord's name (10:16–25). Two events leave a bitter taste of things to come for true followers of Jesus: the rejection of Jesus in his hometown, and the execution of John the Baptist. Instead of being deterred, genuine disciples are made more determined by challenging events such as these.

A Canaanite Woman

Matthew 15:21–28 is a troubling passage, because Jesus seems dismissive of a person in need, with the apparent reason being that she is a female and a non-Jew. We tend to think of Jesus as one who challenged unjust prejudices. Here he seems to be mirroring them. The woman addresses Jesus as "Lord" and does homage to him in much the same way as the Gentile magi had done (2:11) and as the disciples also do to their Lord (14:33). Why does he not respond immediately and graciously to her request? Some scholars seek to soften Jesus' harshness in the passage by theorizing that Jesus planned all along to grant the woman's request. He extended their conversation to test her faith. His intention in the saying "It is not fair to take the children's food and throw it to the dogs" was to mean something like "Charity begins at home."

Still the interchange is troubling. Several features of her interchange with Jesus strike us as demeaning to the woman. His use of the metaphor of dogs, although common among Jews in speaking of Gentiles, is nonetheless unflattering. The healing of the woman's daughter seems to hinge on the woman's ability to think of a quick comeback to Jesus. She is not granted her desire for healing until she recognizes her place as second class to the Jews.

> Was Jesus making a pun? The normal words for woman and dog rhyme in Greek (though here a diminutive form is used, meaning "little dogs").

Despite these troubling aspects, the story cannot be discounted just because we don't like the way Jesus is portrayed. Indeed, a couple of factors make this story consistent with other aspects of the life of Jesus. Sometimes Jesus spoke harshly to people when necessary

(8:22), and Jesus does limit his mission and message to the house of Israel (10:5b–6).

At the same time, Jesus does come into contact with Gentiles, and he does heal them. Several other episodes in Matthew's Gospel imply that Gentiles, as well as Jews, are recipients of Jesus' ministry, and that eventually the gospel will be extended to all people. Note the healing of the centurion's servant (8:5–13) and the exorcism of the Gadarene demoniacs (8:28–34). To remind his mixed Jewish and Gentile church that Jesus had ministered to Gentiles was important to Matthew.

When compared with Mark 7:24–30, Matthew's version of this story heightens the reluctance on the part of Jesus and his disciples to heal the woman's daughter and emphasizes her aggressive pursuit of that healing. Perhaps the story was a vehicle for Matthew to guide his predominantly Jewish-Christian church toward welcoming Gentile members into its fellowship.

Jesus initially ignores the woman's plea, and the disciples urge him to brush her off: "Send her away, for she keeps shouting after us" (15:23). Jesus states explicitly that his mission was to Jews and not to the Gentiles: "I was sent only to the lost sheep of the house of Israel" (15:24). Those verses probably represent those in Matthew's church who were opposed to, or did not understand, the entry of Gentiles into the church.

Matthew stressed the hostility that existed between the woman's ethnic origin and that of the Jews. In Mark, the woman is identified as "a Gentile of Syrophoenician origin" (Mark 7:26). Matthew suggests that she belongs, not to the Greek-influenced population of

> ". . . and never seek their [the Canaanites'] peace or prosperity." —Ezra 9:12

Tyre and Sidon, but to the rural people. She was a Canaanite, a member of a despised population with whom Israel was not supposed to have any dealings (Ezra 9:1–12).

Matthew emphasizes that the woman took the initiative. Instead of relying on a chance meeting, the woman leaves her native land intentionally to come out to meet Jesus. In Mark's version, Jesus goes to her region, and the meeting seems more accidental. The combination of the hostility the Jews would have felt for her as a Canaanite and the courage she showed in coming out to meet Jesus in spite of that hostility depicts her as both active and courageous.

A Woman of Great Faith

Matthew also emphasizes the role of the woman's faith in the healing of her daughter. In contrast to Mark's "For saying that, you may go—the demon has left your daughter" (Mark 7:29), Matthew has "Woman, great is your faith! Let it be done for you as you wish" (15:28). In contrast to the disciples, who show little faith in the stormy boat (8:26), this woman has great faith in equally hostile conditions.

Matthew's opening genealogy listed several people who took the initiative, acted against the accepted social or religious convention, and sought justice. By their actions they furthered the divine plan and embodied a righteousness that takes the form of active faith, so cherished by Matthew. The Canaanite woman belongs in their esteemed company. She shows courage and initiative in coming out to meet Jesus. Her faith and ingenuity are portrayed in an extended conversation with Jesus. She is not identified as fitting a socially expected niche for women of her day. She is not said to be acting under the authority or protection of a husband. Rather, she acts freely and courageously against social and religious convention.

> The woman is described with two words that include the adjective meaning "great." The disciples are described with only one word, with the adjective being combined with the noun to mean "little faith."

She addresses Jesus as "Son of David," providing a sharp contrast between a believing Gentile and the unbelieving Pharisees and scribes from Jerusalem, who are mentioned in the preceding passage. In calling him Son of David, she reminds the readers who Jesus is. (She may be offering a barbed reminder to Jesus as well!) In Matthew's Gospel, the messianic title Son of David occurs in the context of miracles and healings. Although the religious establishment does not hail Jesus as such, this Gentile woman (15:22), the blind (9:27; 20:30–31), and some children do

> "And her daughter was healed instantly" (Matt. 5:28). Jesus performs a long-distance miracle, and it happens *instantly*. The kingdom of God is now, this instant, in Jesus. This phrase is unique to Matthew (cf. 8:13; 9:22; 17:18).

(21:15). If miracles are a demonstration of Jesus' messiahship (Luz, 72), then by connecting this title with Jesus' liberations of the poor and sick, Matthew communicates that Jesus is a Messiah who overturns the normal expectation of a political liberator. This Son of

David liberates simple people from disease and material want.

Matthew wants his readers to regard the Canaanite woman as a prototype of the Gentile believers now seeking to join the church. The image of bread for the gifts God has to offer might refer to the two feeding narratives in Matthew's Gospel, and the parable of the leaven (13:33). In all three instances, God wills that society's vulnerable, the women and children, be fed both physically and spiritually. The bread serves as a positive symbol in contrast to the leaven of the Pharisees and Sadducees.

Some commentators have praised the woman's humility as an encouragement to be humble in the realization that no one deserves the gifts of God in Christ. The focus of the text, however, seems to be on the woman's boldness rather than her humility. She has a desperate need and a deep faith in Jesus. She is in no mood to hear reasons why the two may not be joined together in a joyful healing. She refuses to accept second-class citizenship in the religious caste system of the day as a reason why her daughter must live a stunted life. She overcomes Jesus' reluctance by focusing on the gifts he has to offer and on the deep need her people have for them. She does not waste time or energy taking offense. She persists, and in desperation her faith sparks boldness and ingenuity in her.

> "Noteworthy in this story is the way Jesus appears to be bested in repartee with the . . . woman. Elsewhere in the Gospels, Jesus uniformly prevails over his opponents. Here the woman has the better of it." —Evelyn and Frank Stagg, *Woman in the World of Jesus*, 114.

Jane Dempsey Douglass, professor of historical theology at Princeton Theological Seminary, tells of visiting a church one Sunday when she was a student in college. She was pleased to see the motto inscribed at the top of the bulletin, "The Doors of This Church Are as Wide as the Kingdom of God." Upon visiting several months later, she noticed that the motto was no longer there. "What happened to the motto that used to be on the bulletin?" she asked the woman sitting next to her. "Oh that," came the reply. "It was taken literally, and some black families started attending, so we thought it best to remove it."

Jesus and the early church struggled with who should be the focus of God's promises, who should be fed first. The church today continues to struggle with that issue, even with a mandate to spread the good news to all the world—quite literally, to make the doors of our churches as wide as the kingdom of God. Like the early church, we continue to be stretched by people on the margins who are faithful and bold enough to speak up for justice for themselves or their families, and in so doing, unleash God's righteousness.

? Questions for Reflection

1. The passages in this unit have been concerned with Jesus' authority over the powers of chaos. What are some similarities between the stories of the calming of the storm and the healing of the woman's daughter? What are some differences in the stories? What was the role of faith in the two stories?

2. With the creeds of the church, we affirm that Jesus was both fully God and fully human. However, this story of the storm at sea sets up a puzzling question about the nature of Jesus and the reality of threats to his life. What are your thoughts as to the degree of harm facing Jesus (and for that matter, the disciples) in the boat in the storm at sea?

3. The healing story was not just about faith. A foreign woman confronts Jesus and negotiates healing for her daughter. What barriers did the woman cross to get what she needed? Many barriers exist today, even between individuals in the same church. How does the woman's example speak to these barriers?

4. Again, there is tension in this story, Jesus does not act in a manner appropriate to the expectations of his day and age. He initially argued, on religious grounds (the prohibition in Ezra is due in part to the Canaanites' worship of other gods), that he should not respond to the woman's request. Then he agreed. What does this story offer to questions of religious differences?

Peter's Confession and Jesus' Passion

Peter's confession and Jesus' passion prediction, along with his teaching about cross bearing, mark a watershed in the plot of Matthew. From this point on there is no turning back for Jesus, for Peter, or for us, if we would be disciples of the Messiah.

The Confession of Peter

Matthew attributes breakthrough significance to Peter's confession, a fundamental and divine revelation of who Jesus is. Peter makes this affirmation about Jesus' identity because God has enabled him to recognize Jesus as "the Messiah, the Son of the living God" (16:16). Jesus answers: "Flesh and blood has not revealed this to you, but my Father in heaven" (16:17).

In contrast to the time line of Mark's Gospel or John's, Jesus "names" Peter at this point. Jesus names Peter "stone," or "rock" (Greek *petros*). In Ephesians (2:20), the apos-

We misrepresent the cross. It was not a piece of jewelry to adorn one's neck, but instead a cruel form of execution.

tles and prophets are together called the foundation of God's household. But here, Peter is marked as the church's foundation. There is a consistent tradition in the New Testament supporting a prominent, or foundational, role for Peter that in Matthew's account begins here at his confession (see Luke 22:32; 24:34; 1 Cor. 15:5; Gal. 1:18).

What does that role really mean? This declaration about Peter in verses 17–19 appears only in Matthew and has many mysterious and bewildering aspects. Some question how the historical Jesus could have spoken this saying. They reason that Jesus could not have anticipated the development of the institutional church after his death and resurrection. Perhaps this verse reflects the influence of Matthew in his speaking to his own church.

The word used for church (*ekklesia*) was used in the Old Testament to refer to "the people of God," "the assembly," or "the congregation." The Essene community at Qumran referred to themselves as a congregation (*ekklesia*), that chose to separate from the corrupt political and religious world in order to be faithful to God's covenant (Hill, 261). So Jesus' calling his followers an *ekklesia* might have referred to the community of the faithful that would persevere in his teachings as his influence lived on following the fate he felt awaited him.

"Gates of Hell [Hades]"

This phrase also appears in the Wisdom of Solomon 16:13. Similar biblical images are found in Job 17:16; Isaiah 38:10; Psalms 9:13; 69:15; and Revelation 20:1. The phrase communicates a picture of a locked gate with bars that separates the power or place of death from the living.

Another bewildering aspect of these verses is Jesus' statement that the gates of Hades will not prevail against the church. The expression is a poetic way of describing the power of death (see Isa. 38:10). The congregation of the new covenant will persevere into the coming age, despite the threatening powers of darkness.

The Keys to the Kingdom

Another question concerns the mysterious "keys of the kingdom of heaven" (16:19) and what Peter is authorized to bind and to loose. Countless jokes and stories depict St. Peter as the gatekeeper of the Pearly Gates; but the keys symbolize Peter's authority, not in the clouds, but in the church. Binding and loosing refer to Peter's authority to enforce the discipline of the church by laying down binding rules or exempting people from them (18:18). Some argue that the church, especially through its ordained leadership, continues to fill and extend the authoritative role Jesus conveys to Peter in this verse, whereas others see the role of Peter as unique in scope and time, not intended as repeatable.

The picture of Peter holding a set of keys invested with the authority to admit or refuse admittance to the kingdom tends toward a negative job description. What about the joyful, invitational function implied in Jesus' words? Another image from Peter's life comes from Acts, where he is the chief missionary of the Easter message. There Peter has the joyful task of leading many into the kingdom through his preaching.

The giving of the keys to Peter allows Matthew to tell his readers that Jesus also invests Peter with authority to invite into the kingdom those previously excluded. In verses 17–19, Matthew could have been sending a message to the conservative Jewish Christians in his congregation who didn't want to admit Gentiles. "We must defer to Peter's authority," Matthew was implying. And his decision (see Acts 10) was to admit Gentiles with open arms. Who can contest the holder of the keys?

> **Why must the knowledge that Jesus is the Messiah be a secret?**
>
> This passage in Matthew is probably drawn from Mark's Gospel. For a thorough discussion, see Schweizer, *The Good News According to Mark*, 54–56. It's interesting to note that in the parallel passage of Luke 9:21, the emphasis of the secret isn't on Jesus' messiahship, but on the fact that the Messiah must die.

Though surrounded by perplexities and questions, Peter's confession is of crucial importance. From it we learn who Jesus is—the Messiah. From it we learn who Peter is and will be: Peter is the one whom God inspires to confess publicly Jesus' identity. Therefore, Peter is the one Jesus chooses to invest with authority in the movement that will grow from his ministry.

The Passion of Jesus

It is also important to note that Peter's confession serves as a springboard from which Jesus makes his first passion prediction. The reader learns through Peter that Jesus is the Messiah, and then learns from Jesus what that messiahship will mean for the future. This passage is the hinge between the Galilean ministry and the Passion. It is a turning point. From here on, Jesus' focus is on preparing his disciples for his death. He repeats this announcement in 17:22–23 and 20:17–29. Verses 24–28 show that Jesus' announcement is not just a prediction of his personal future. The invitation to his followers, including us, is to find their identity by participating in that future. In a real sense, Jesus and Peter name each other. In that mutual naming, they challenge us as to our allegiance and identity. We can no longer plead ignorance. We too know who Jesus is. The question becomes, "Knowing now where the winding path will lead, will we follow him?"

> "Christianity never consists in *knowing about Jesus;* it always consists in *knowing Jesus.*" —William Barclay, *The Gospel of Matthew,* Daily Study Bible, vol. 2, p. 138.

If Peter had not just been praised and entrusted with great future authority by Jesus, his rebuke (v. 23) might not appear quite so harsh. From holder of the keys to mouthpiece of Satan! From rock to stumbling block? In Peter's defense, Jesus hasn't yet helped him understand the "why" question. Jesus has affirmed that this grim future must happen, but he has not backed up that strange statement with reasons. No one wants pain and suffering to befall a loved one. Peter's impulse is perfectly understandable. In fact, shouldn't Jesus have been flattered that a key follower cared this much about him? Why doesn't Jesus thank him and then gently correct him?

Perhaps resistance to his own future had been percolating within Jesus' thoughts. When Peter voices opposition, Jesus recognizes its source—his old nemesis from chapter 4. Because Satan couldn't get anywhere with Jesus, that old devil trys to erode the devotion of the disciples. Peter's sentiments must be sternly condemned. If left unrestrained, Jesus' followers might block the desire of Jesus to go it alone, and they might actively oppose his mission as well. The lack of trust Peter shows in Jesus is doubly disturbing in light of the tremendous trust Jesus has just placed in him.

This is the first inkling of Peter's complex character, and of his own troubled waters that lie ahead. Peter fulfills a unique role in the early church, but at the same time he represents all would-be disciples. Every one of us combines the potential to believe and serve with the potential to abscond and abandon. This moment foreshadows Peter's threefold betrayal on the night of Jesus' trial. This moment also points toward the faith and leadership Peter embodied for the early church. For Peter and for us, whatever our past relationship has been with Jesus, forgiveness brings a fresh start. A high calling beckons, but severe trials lie ahead. For Peter and for us, the good news offered to others is also the good news to live by: the news that

Christ offers strength and joy to accomplish the most difficult of ministries.

Bearing a Cross

Jesus' teaching on cross bearing is the substance of the disciple's life. This teaching is addressed to Peter, to the disciples, and to us. This teaching answers the "why" question: "Why will Jesus suffer and die?" The answer is because of the risky way he chose to live, his commitment to be a doer and not just a hearer. Jesus summed up his chosen way of life with this saying, "For those who want to save their life will lose it, and those who lose their life for my sake will find it" (16:25).

This saying directly contradicts the traditional wisdom that we find in the book of Proverbs. There young people were taught how to preserve, secure, and extend their lives by hard work, moderation in food and drink, avoiding foolish people, knowing when to keep quiet, and planning for the future. The reward promised them was long life, health, many children, and a good reputation among their peers (Prov. 16:17).

This saying about finding and losing represents Jesus' risky subversive wisdom. He talked when he should have kept quiet. He offended powerful people whom he should have cultivated. He cultivated powerless people who could do nothing to advance his career. He gave up the emotional and physical comforts of home to live an insecure, itinerant existence in which he had nowhere to lay his head (8:20). A contemporary version of traditional wisdom is the familiar saying "Finders keepers, losers weepers." Jesus' version was "Finders weepers, losers keepers!"

> "Cross bearers forfeit the game of power before the first inning; they are never selected as 'most .likely to succeed.' Cross bearers are dropouts in the school of self-promotion. They do not pick up their crosses as a means for personal fulfillment, career advancement, or self-expression."
> —Thomas G. Long, *Matthew*, Westminster Bible Companion, 190.

For Jesus, this risky life that culminated in the cross was a choice made out of commitment to his convictions about God's mission for him. As his ministry progressed and opposition to his teaching grew, Jesus suspected that his opponents would not let him live. The predictions of his death to his disciples, which occur several times throughout the Gospel, indicate both his growing foreboding and his mounting determination. Jesus, knowing what awaited him in Jerusalem, continued to journey toward it. Why?

As a human being, Jesus had a choice—to accept the sacrifice of the cross or to avoid it. Jesus chose to risk the cross, not out of a life-denying asceticism that elevates self-denial for suffering's sake. Nor did he eagerly seek death out of a desire for martyrdom that might assure him the admiration of future generations. Nor did he believe that God wanted to punish him or that being abused by others was inherently a good thing. He accepted the cross out of his radical love for God and for others. Having been courageous and outspoken in his convictions throughout his life, he saw no other path with integrity than to continue the race of faith into the Valley of the Shadow of Death.

The reasons why Jesus underwent the pain and humiliation of the cross can be misunderstood. The meaning of a cross in our lives is misunderstood also. Too often the cross has been defined as oppression by others. Women in situations of domestic violence, who have gone to their pastors for advice, have been assured wrongly, "It's your cross, sister. You must bear it, because it's your cross." Slaves were told by white preachers that slavery was the cross the Lord wanted them to bear. Too casually, the cross is defined as an everyday nuisance that has to be tolerated. Hearing things like "The one-hour commute to work is my cross to bear" or "Weeding is my cross to bear for having a garden" trivializes Jesus' teaching beyond recognition.

Self-denial is misunderstood as well. Too often in the history of Christianity, self-denial has meant condemning the body and its appetites. Based on a false separation of body and spirit, this condemnation continues to lead to extremes of asceticism that harm physical health or denigrate God's good gift of sexuality. This misunderstanding runs counter to the tradition of the Hebrew Scriptures that God created both the world and human beings, and called them good.

Misunderstanding self-denial has meant for some not to pursue any dreams or talents that bring pleasure in life. It is like saying, "Since you love acting, you must become a lawyer," or like the tongue-in-cheek dieter's dictum: "If it tastes good, spit it out."

Automatically subordinating the needs and dreams of self to those of others is another misunderstanding of self-denial. Theologians in recent years have pointed out that many women are kept from serving God fully and joyfully because they have an underdeveloped sense of self, a lack of confidence in their God-given talents. For a number of reasons, many women feel guilty about setting boundaries that allow the time and energy to be good stewards of their mental, emotional, spiritual, and physical health. Instead, they allow the demands of others to rule them. The result is a diminished sense of their own identity as children of God, and a stifling of their contributions to God's kingdom.

For both men and women, Jesus' teachings in verses 24–26 call not for self-effacement but for affirmation of oneself as a child of God. This saying must be set in the context of Jesus' command about loving others. He did not say, "Thou shalt love others and not thyself," but rather that we are to love others as we love ourselves (22:39). There will come times, of course, when in choosing to follow Christ, we risk the loss of a stable life in familiar surroundings, of relationships, career advancement, the approval of others, and material comforts. We may be lonely, disapproved of, frightened, and threatened. But we must be clear, as Jesus was, that we risk these losses out of radical love for God and not out of a deep-seated hatred for ourselves.

> **Want to Know More?**
>
> **About asceticism?** See Donald K. McKim, *Westminster Dictionary of Theological Terms* (Louisville, Ky.: Westminster John Knox Press, 1996), 19; Richard P. McBrien, ed. *The HarperCollins Encyclopedia of Catholicism* (San Francisco: HarperSanFrancisco, 1995), 100.
>
> **About apostolic authority or succession?** See Alan Richardson and John Bowden, *The Westminster Dictionary of Christian Theology* (Philadelphia: Westminster Press, 1983), 33–36.
>
> **About the concept of martyrdom?** See Richardson and Bowden, *The Westminster Dictionary of Christian Theology*, 347–49.

Questions for Reflection

1. In this passage, Simon identifies Jesus, and Jesus names Simon. This poses a challenge to us. How do you identify Jesus? What do those identifications mean to you in your life? If Jesus could give you a nickname, what might it be?
2. In rapid succession, Peter has the unenviable position of being first the rock of the church, and then the agent of Satan. Perhaps there is only a fine line between the two. What helps make the distinction between the two?
3. These passages are a turning point in Matthew's Gospel. Though the activity of Jesus continues to involve healings and teachings,

all of his subsequent actions and sayings are viewed through the lens of his predicted death. What have been some turning points in your life, moments that forever changed the way you viewed things?

4. Verses 24–28 offer words of both warning and promise. What are some of those warnings and promises?

Rewards and Grace

In chapter 17, Jesus takes his inner circle of disciples up a high mountain. His face shines like the sun, a reminder of Moses' face, which also shone after he had talked with God (Ex. 34:29–35). The face of Jesus reflects God's glory, which confirms his messiahship and echoes the divine words of his baptismal experience: "This is my Son, the Beloved; with him I am well pleased; listen to him!" (17:5).

The disciples, despite their desire to stay on the mountain and revel in the experience, follow Jesus down the mountain into the needy crowd. There Jesus cures a boy with a demon and chastises the disciples who could not do the job because of their little faith. He then engages in a series of teaching moments that include the parable of the lost sheep (18:10–14), the parable of the unforgiving servant (18:23–35), a confrontation with the Pharisees about divorce (19:3–12), and the discussion of rewards and grace.

Leaving Everything

"Look, we have left everything and followed you. What then will we have?" (19:27). It's an honest question, and a good one, even with Jesus' explanation in chapter 16 that those who lose their lives will find them. To be fair to the disciples, at this point in their journey with Jesus, what they have given up may be much clearer to them than any gains that may lie before them. Peter and the others probably miss their children and

> "For those who want to save their life will lose it, and those who lose their life for my sake will find it." —Matthew 16:25

extended families, yearn for their wives, and crave the familiar surroundings of their beds, boats, and nets.

In the encounter between Jesus and the rich young man
(19:16–22), the disciples have just seen someone who kept all those
things and has lots of money besides. The young man considers giving them up to follow Jesus but decides not to. Jesus then taught that
a camel could go through the eye of a needle more easily than a rich
person could get into heaven. At first these are words of comfort.
The disciples, being spiritually svelte because they have given up
their possessions to follow Jesus, feel assured that they will fit
through the eye of the needle. Then Jesus adds these disturbing
words: "but for God all things are possible" (19:26).

If I were a disciple standing there, I would have thought, "Wait a
minute! You mean even someone who has not given up anything, or
who gives up wealth late in life, may be able to get into the kingdom?" Didn't the emperor Constantine put off his baptism until his
death, so that he could sin with impunity? And didn't Augustine cry
out to God, "Lord, make me chaste, but not today"? It's nice that
God is so merciful, but what about those who embark on their career in righteousness earlier in life? Isn't there something extra for
them?

Peter voices the disciples' demand for just compensation. Jesus assures him that he and the disciples will be rewarded with roles of responsibility in the kingdom to come. When the Son of Man comes,
the disciples will share in his rule over the new age. Though the clar-
ification of that rule is not spelled out, they are promised a glorious
future in the age to come. Jesus continues and makes a general statement about recompense for anyone who has left relationships and
possessions to follow him (see also 10:40–42). Then comes an ambiguous "great reversal" statement: "Many who are first will be last,
and the last will be first" (19:30).

About whom is Jesus speaking here? He is talking partly about the
rich young man and those like him. In this age, the rich are first. If
they don't change their way of life, in the coming kingdom the rich
will be last. But the saying is addressed to the disciples as both a
word of comfort and a word of challenge. The words give comfort if
the disciples want to compare themselves to the rich young man.
Jesus is saying to his disciples, "Though that young man is enjoying
his earthly luxuries, you have a promise for a future realm."

The reversal saying challenges the disciples in their attitudes toward women, children, and other "unimportant" people with whom

Jesus chose to mingle, heal, and share meals. When the disciples heard this strange saying about reversal of status, they probably identified with the last who would become first. But Jesus used the saying to caution them lest *they* become the first who would be last. Jesus' followers are to beware a spiritual arrogance by which they consider themselves to be the self-appointed elite and others to be of lower degree. On two earlier occasions in Matthew, the disciples tried to keep people from bothering Jesus—the Canaanite woman (15:23) and a group of children (19:13). Later, their arrogance and ambition become clear when James and John send their mother to negotiate for the corner offices in the kingdom of heaven (20:20–28).

Jesus and his disciples were a group of people on the margins of society, voluntary have-nots, looked on with suspicion and derision by society's power brokers. Jesus called them to be, as biblical scholar Elisabeth Schüssler Fiorenza has aptly said, "a discipleship of equals." In an ironic twist, the disciples discard equality and try to duplicate the hierarchical relationships of the political and religious establishment. They jockey for positions closest to Jesus and ask in their hearts, "Which of us is the greatest?" Jesus tells them that although some will have leadership roles, all are equal in the love of God. Like the equality of lay and clergy in a contemporary expression of this ideal, all have equal status. Clergy are ordained to a special function within the body of Christ, but ordination is to service, not to status.

> "He is no fool, who gives what he cannot keep, to gain what he cannot lose." —Jim Elliot, as quoted by Elizabeth Elliot in *Shadow of the Almighty: The Life and Testament of Jim Elliot* (New York: Harper & Brothers, 1958), 108.

The disciples will receive a reward for what they have given up, but they are not the only ones. Everyone who sacrifices family relationships or property for Jesus' sake will be rewarded a hundredfold and inherit eternal life (19:29), the very gift the rich young man craved from Jesus (19:16). To be told that the first shall become last is to be told not to place one's self above others because of a larger sacrifice or an earlier sacrifice. Whether rich or poor, whether new or longtime disciples, whether adults or children, whether men or women, we are to take Jesus' words from the Beatitudes to heart: "Blessed are the poor in spirit, for theirs is the kingdom of heaven" (5:3). We are to remember humbly our need for God, in a constant turning to God for strength and guidance that alone can make us "pure in heart."

The Vineyard Laborers

Parables are a favorite teaching device of Jesus. Parables were popular with rabbis and have a few uses in the Hebrew Scriptures (see Judg. 9:7–15; 2 Sam. 12:1–15). Parables are short narrative fictions that employ metaphor to spark insights about a spiritual truth. Matthew's parables generally focus on the theme of the kingdom of God—on the kinds of preparation for the final advent that will number the righteous among the sheep, not the goats.

In a parable, the story Jesus tells sounds familiar at first but usually contains a twist—for example, a small portion of seed yields an astronomical harvest. Someone who deserves to be censured gets greeted with open arms and a fatted calf dinner. Something is askew, something is foreign to the expected way of thinking and acting. Something is out of kilter, and often, that something is how the kingdom of God turns this familiar world upside down.

> The Greek word *parabole* means literally "a throwing alongside." Parables are stories, phrases, or images that place unlikely things beside each other to draw comparisons in one or more ways. For more reading on the parables of Jesus, see William Barclay, *And Jesus Said: A Handbook on the Parables of Jesus* (Philadelphia: Westminster Press, 1970), and Robert Stein, *An Introduction to the Parables of Jesus* (Philadelphia: Westminster Press, 1981).

The parable of the workers in the vineyard declares the sovereign grace and goodwill of God, who welcomes "latecomers" into the kingdom. This parable, which is preceded by and ends with the statement that the first and last will switch places, is addressed to those who criticized the acceptance of outcasts into the kingdom of God. The contemporaries of Jesus, members of Matthew's church, and even we, should listen to the several meanings of this parable.

> Even today, we harbor ill feelings about taxes and tax collectors. The reasons for distrust of tax collectors in Jesus' day are complex. For a good discussion, see Paul J. Achtemeier, ed., *Harper's Bible Dictionary* (San Francisco: Harper & Row, 1985), 841.

Jesus probably used the parable to support his choice to associate with tax collectors and sinners. Even though these people had come late in life to their service of God, they would be accepted into the kingdom. He is not teaching an economic principle but rather a spiritual principle. The owner claims the right to pay the workers, not on the basis of their merits, but on the basis of his own compassion. Those who worship a God of compassion should imitate his generosity, not begrudge it.

For Jesus, the parable teaches that eternal life is not the reward of human merit but a free gift. The sacrifices of the followers of Jesus indeed will be honored by God. That reward, however, will be so much larger than their sacrifices that it can only be a gift of sheer grace, something God gives that cannot be earned or compelled by effort. Paul affirms this overwhelming discrepancy when he writes: "I consider that the sufferings of this present time are not worth comparing with the glory about to be revealed to us" (Rom. 8:18). Though some followers of Jesus may feel their long, costly service qualifies them for a higher rate of pay in the kingdom, all must humbly acknowledge that they are like the eleventh-hour workers. No one deserves the glorious future that God has prepared for us.

Matthew uses Jesus' parable to speak to his context. The vineyard is a familiar image from the Old Testament to refer to Israel (Isa. 5:1). For Matthew, the vineyard is the Christian community. Those who join late are treated as equal in privilege to those who joined early. This parable parallels that of the prodigal son in Luke 15: the grumbling of the full-day workers parallels the grumbling of the elder brother. Matthew 20:15 literally asks, "Is your eye evil?" (see NRSV footnote). The eye was often referred to with the sense of an attitude of grudging, envy, or jealousy (1 Sam. 2:29; Eccl. 1:8).

A vineyard in Israel today

The parable challenged Jesus' disciples in their spiritual arrogance. The church of Matthew's day was challenged because some Jewish Christians opposed the entry of Gentiles into the blessings of the kingdom. Today in our churches, we are challenged by this parable when we begrudge the joy of the gospel to those whom we deem less industrious, less committed, or less worthy than we are.

The character(s) with whom we identify in a story tells a great deal about ourselves and our self-conceptions. I suspect that many of us identify with the workers who started out early in the morning and so, on grounds of economic fairness, we feel uncomfortable with this parable. Perhaps we ought to identify with those who started last. What if we were the ones who butted in line and got something for nothing? Only when we shed our spiritual arrogance can we celebrate the good news of this quirky parable rather than be offended by its economics. The generosity of God reverses our way of thinking.

> "Joyous participation in God's kingdom, with trust that the outcome will depend more on the generosity of the 'householder' than on the amount of work by the laborer, is preferable to a mere contractual relationship that easily breeds resentment against those who seem to deserve less."
> —R. David Kaylor, *Jesus the Prophet: His Vision of the Kingdom on Earth* (Louisville, Ky.: Westminster John Knox Press, 1994), 130.

When the father of a church member died, the pastor was asked to conduct the funeral. Not knowing Bill as well as she did Bill's family, the pastor met with the family to learn about this man. Bill had been a vital individual with a good sense of humor. He had been a successful salesman and had made an excellent living, enjoying his retirement and frequent golf games until he was stricken with Alzheimer's disease two years before.

Sitting around a kitchen table one Saturday afternoon, Bill's children, their spouses, and even a niece and nephew described their loved one. The pastor began by asking, "If you could express in one sentence what you learned from Bill, what would it be?" Nobody had to think about the question very long. "Give without counting the cost and without expecting a return," one of them said quickly. That sentiment was echoed all around the table. Then they started giving examples. "He put me through school," said his niece. "I didn't even ask; he just knew my folks couldn't do it." "He bailed me out of jail," said his son. "He never gave up hope in me," said his nephew. "He gave me the gift of somebody believing in me."

Want to Know More?

About day laborers? See William R. Herzog II, *Parables as Subversive Speech: Jesus as Pedagogue of the Oppressed* (Louisville, Ky.: Westminster John Knox Press, 1994), 88–90.

About farming in the time of Jesus? See Paul J. Achtemeier, ed., *Harper's Bible Dictionary* (San Francisco: Harper & Row, 1985), 303–4.

One after the other offered stories about a man who knew how to give without counting the cost, without expecting a return. "He always made sure his children's needs were met," his daughter said, "but sometimes, I admit we felt jealous when he would give time and money to people who weren't in our immediate family. Now I realize that his example of generosity was his greatest gift to us."

One came away from that kitchen table feeling humbled and instructed about the subject of generosity.

? Questions for Reflection

1. Peter comments that the disciples have left everything to follow Jesus, and they expect a reward. What are the sacrifices of faith? What are the rewards of faith? What influence does the possibility of reward have on your decisions about personal sacrifice?
2. As an introduction to the parable in this passage, verse 29 refers to "hundredfold" and calls to mind the parable of the sower (13:1–9). What are some of the similarities between these two parables?
3. When asked what was the lesson of this parable, one student responded, "Be last." Most of our schooling and work experiences are based on a rewards system—the more the work, the greater the reward. How do you reconcile the teaching of this parable with your experiences within a reward system?
4. This parable offers many lessons, two of which are issues about privilege and trust. Who is in the position of privilege, the laborers or the landowner? Why? Who best exemplifies trust, the laborers or the landowner? Why?

8 Matthew 22:1–14

The Parable of the King's Wedding Banquet

At first glance, this is an upsetting and unpleasant parable, a brutal story with terrific mood swings. A king's son is going to be married, and the mood is happy. The king throws a banquet, and the mood is happier still. When all of the invited guests say "No," the mood shifts downward, toward sadness. Then, shockingly, all of the invited guests are slaughtered, and the mood becomes dire. We are aghast and mortified! Next, the poor and the outcast get invited to the banquet, and the mood moves tentatively upward. But one of the guests is caught without a proper wedding garment and is cast out of the party. Swiftly, the mood falls to the depths, sweeping us to a place of outer darkness.

In the context of Jesus' ministry in Matthew, however, the parable is less about mood swings and more about the complex theological idea of God's judgment. In what is now the last week of his life, Jesus is in the Temple, where the religious authorities challenge his authority (21:23–27), and he responds with three parables about judgment. The first is about two sons (21:28–32); it contrasts the religious establishment, the "insiders" who reject Jesus, with the social outcasts, the "outsiders" who accept Jesus. The son who said "Yes" but did not go represents those priests and lawyers whose actions did not fit their public professions of piety. The son who said "No" but then repented represents the tax collectors and sinners who have responded to Jesus.

> "Let your 'Yes' be yes and your 'No' be no." —James 5:12

The second parable is about wicked tenants (21:33–44). In Matthew's presentation, this is an allegory reminiscent of a similar

76

allegory in Isaiah 5. In this parable, the tenants who kill the landowner's son symbolize the leaders of Israel, and the landowner's son symbolizes Jesus. This parable ends with a threat to remove the wicked tenants, to punish them, and to give the vineyard to others. This implied charge by Jesus against the religious leaders alienates them even more. In fact, the wrath of the religious leaders boils into what later becomes the plot to arrest Jesus. (This passage should be treated with great care by Christians. What began as a prophetic critique by a Jew to fellow Jews, a critique designed to provoke repentance and not to condemn, has been used wrongfully to fuel the fires of anti-Semitism. As Christians we do well to focus, not so much on what the parable says about the Jews, but on its implications for Christians. If the "others" of verse 41 are to be understood as the church, then Christians now are the tenants and, thus, accountable to the owner and charged with producing the fruits of the kingdom [verse 43].)

The Banquet

The third parable, the story of the king's wedding banquet, continues the theme of the first two parables—God's judgment upon those who reject Jesus as Messiah. The parable involves a banquet, which stands as a powerful religious symbol. The Jews of Jesus' day believed that at the end time the Messiah would come and gather God's people around a banquet table; this idea of the Messiah's banquet was a popular theological notion in Matthew's day. The early Christians believed that Jesus had already begun the Messiah's banquet during his ministry when he ate and drank with sinners. Indeed, when the early church celebrated the Lord's Supper, they believed they were participating in that messianic banquet.

The details of the parable reflect the customary etiquette for banquet hosts in that time. Guests were invited to the banquet well ahead of time and were expected to send word of their acceptance. Then, when the banquet arrangements were complete and the meal was ready, messengers were sent to let the guests know that now was the time to come. In Matthew's scheme of things, the first invited guests were the Jews.

> "Score a sad point, the unhappy truth is the world is full of fools who won't believe a good thing when they hear it." —Robert Farrar Capon, *The Parables of Judgment* (Grand Rapids: Wm. B. Eerdmans Publishing Co., 1989), 121.

But the first guests refused to come to the banquet, some with violent contempt, so the host moved to the B list of guests, who were gathered in from the streets. (Matthew interpreted the destruction of Jerusalem by the Romans in A.D. 70 as God's punishment for the rejection of Jesus as Messiah. Hence the reference to the burning city in verse 7.) The B list of guests included those judged unworthy by everyone else; the Romans referred to them as "the expendables"—the poor, prostitutes, and tax collectors. Again, for Matthew these were probably understood to be Gentiles. Once these "expendables" believed in Jesus, they repented of what was past and bore the fruits of their belief by showing deeds of love to one another.

When the privileged guests, those first on the list, refuse at the last minute to come to the banquet, they lose their places of honor and move from first to last. The common folk off the street, digging in the garbage for food, who don't get invited to many parties, get called in from the streets to come to the king's party. Thus the last become the first. And they all come. Matthew says, "The wedding hall was filled with guests" (22:10). Why couldn't Matthew have left it at that—with a happy ending, as Luke's account does (Luke 14:15–24)?

The Wedding Garment

Matthew's version of this parable ruins the "last become first" happy ending by adding a disturbing plot twist. In Matthew's account the street people are all partying. There is the smell of terrific hors d'oeuvres; there are the sounds of raucous laughter and music made for dancing. As readers, we're prepared to step in and join this party. Then the king comes sweeping in and spots this unlucky guy not wearing a wedding robe. The music changes into an ominous minor key. Before our horrified eyes, the king, whom we thought was a gracious host, verbally assaults the man for not being properly attired. Worse yet, he has him thrown out, bound and gagged. Then we hear the usual sound effects Matthew uses in his judgment parables: weeping and gnashing of teeth. What is happening here? Has the host bared some fangs beneath his smile and revealed himself to be a malicious bouncer?

How, we want to know, can someone brought into the wedding hall from off the street be expected to have a wedding garment? And why all the hoopla about coming to the banquet improperly attired anyway? Aren't things like status and clothing unimportant in the kingdom of God? What if a minister forgot to wear the proper clerical robe? Would that minister be bound, gagged, and stuffed in the coat closet in the narthex while the service proceeded? Hardly. Why should the king get away with this behavior?

Some suggest that the episode about the garment (vv. 11–14) is a fragment of another parable whose beginning was lost, and Matthew tacked it on to the end of this one. It is tempting to bounce Matthew's thorny last four verses of the parable out on their ear. We would do so except that Matthew has a habit of sticking a zinger in at the end of a passage— a zinger that on the surface seems like bad news, but upon a second glance, might be good news. Maybe that's the case here. Maybe there is good news.

Maybe the "wedding garment" is not meant to be taken literally. The garment may instead be a symbol, a metaphor for the faithfulness and obedience God expects of those who are members of the kingdom. If so, the wedding garment stands for the willingness of those invited to the banquet to bear the fruits of the kingdom. The wedding garment reveals a spirit of faithful obedience to the banquet host. In this understanding, the need for a proper garment explains the excuses the first invited wedding guests gave for not attending. They knew that if they came they would have to put on a wedding gar-

> **". . . into the outer darkness, where there will be weeping and gnashing of teeth" (Matt. 22:13).**
>
> This phrase or a variation appears frequently in Matthew (cf. 8:12; 13:42; 13:50; 24:51; 25:30). It presumes a location for the doomed and is perhaps borrowed from other ancient concepts of an afterlife and time of eternal judgment. In other writings, the place of torment is described as "darkness" (cf. *1 Enoch* 103:8; *Psalms of Solomon* 14:9; 15:10; *Sibylline Oracles* 2:292). Elsewhere, the dead travel through several spheres of heaven, passing through levels of darkness, ice, demons, and so forth, before arriving in the innermost seventh sphere, which is illuminated by God (cf. *Questions of Ezra* 16–21; *Testament of Levi* 3:2; *2 Enoch* 7:2; *Apocalypse of Paul* 42). Though elsewhere in the Bible "gnashing of teeth" has the sense of rage-filled grinding teeth (cf. Pss. 35:16; 37:12; 112:10; Lam. 2:16), here the phrase may communicate shivering or chattering teeth because of the icy cold and great distance from the light of God. In the absence of a precise meaning, the phrase still communicates a mournful, painful separation from the joyful comfort of God's kingdom.

ment, and they didn't want to. They lacked respect for the king and his authority in issuing the invitation, and, busy with trivial pursuits, they broke their commitment to come to his banquet. So the invitation went out to the street people instead.

In this understanding, the parable reveals what happened in Jesus' earthly ministry. Many of the Gentiles flocked to the Messiah's banquet table. Many crowds followed him, wanting his miracles, his healing, or a full stomach. Many came to the banquet, but not all were willing to use that nourishment as energy for faithful discipleship. One could show up without a wedding garment—without a genuine respect for the Lord of the banquet or without an attitude of faithful obedience.

"He is the recipient of massive grace. Where is his awe? Where is his wonder? Where is his regard for generosity? . . . Here he is bellying up to the punch bowl, stuffing his mouth with fig preserves, and wiping his hands on his T-shirt. . . . In his self-absorption, he hadn't the foggiest idea . . . that he was at a wedding banquet at all. . . . [He could not] tell the difference between the wedding feast of the Lamb of God and happy hour in a bus station bar." —Thomas G. Long, *Matthew*, Westminster Bible Companion, 248.

Thematic to Matthew's entire Gospel is the insistence that God's gracious invitation needs to be met by our committed response. Matthew stresses this message of genuine righteousness again and again in the Gospel. It is individuals who know their need for God who will be a part of the kingdom. "Blessed are the poor in spirit, for theirs is the kingdom of heaven" (5:3). The hard news is that, although everyone is invited, everyone has to show up wearing a wedding garment. The good news is that everyone is invited, and that anyone who shows up wearing a wedding garment, whether invited first or last, will enjoy the blessings of the Messiah's banquet.

One cannot make light of the moment as the first invited guests did, and as the garmentless guest did. The response to the invitation is critical. Matthew casts this parable after two other parables whose stern message is on obedience and genuine righteousness—a warning that the believer must both speak and act righteously.

What does it mean to be a friend of Jesus?

In the parable of the workers in the vineyard, the landowner addresses the complaining laborer as "friend" (Matt. 20:13). Later in 26:50, Jesus calls Judas "friend" in the garden of his betrayal. As is the case here, neither of these two characters is cast in a favorable light. Robert Capon suggested the appropriate understanding would be "Buster." —Robert Farrar Capon, *The Parables of Judgment* (Grand Rapids: Wm. B. Eerdmans Publishing Co., 1989), 124.

The invitation is continually being extended. The Lord of the banquet is continually sending out messengers. They come in the form of other people, of circumstances, and of our own inward insights countless times each day. We are being barraged by the invitation to set aside our trivial pursuits. We are being invited to lay aside our sorrow, our sense of unworthiness, our complacent view of life where all is right with the world as long as our families are comfortable. These are not reasons to stay away but are signs of how desperately we need to put on the wedding garment and come to the banquet. And as we come, we are to bring those who weep in the darkness back to the banquet table where there is always room and nourishment for one more.

This passage calls us to reflect on the questions: What is it that keeps us from answering God's call to enter into the joy of the kingdom banquet? Why do we exclude ourselves from the banquet of joy to which we are called by God in Christ? Why do we exclude others? How can the banquet be enjoyed unless the hall is full?

The parable warns us about reversals of fortune and of preparedness for the kingdom. It also surprises us with its wide-open and far-reaching sense of invitation. All are invited, including the dregs of society, the good and the bad.

Want to Know More?

About banquets? See Paul J. Achtemeier, ed., *Harper's Bible Dictionary* (San Francisco: Harper & Row, 1985), 91–92.

About the concept of judgment? See Donald K. McKim, *Westminster Dictionary of Theological Terms* (Louisville, Ky.: Westminster John Knox Press, 1996), 151; Shirley C. Guthrie, *Christian Doctrine*, rev. ed. (Louisville, Ky.: Westminster John Knox Press, 1994), 387–89.

A story is told about Judas Iscariot. Judas, we remember, left the Last Supper early and betrayed Christ. Then Judas found himself face down at the bottom of a deep, dark well. He lay there for what seemed an eternity. Finally, he turned himself over. With his face now turned up, he noticed a pinhole of light way above him. Slowly, gingerly, he pulled himself up along the sides of the well, heading toward the light. Sometimes he would slip and fall back, and it would take another eternity to recover his strength to go on. But as he drew closer to the light, he grew stronger, and he slipped less often. Finally, after what can only be described as an eternity of eternities, he pulled himself through the opening of the well. To his amazement, he found that he was in a room with a young rabbi, who was hosting a supper for some friends. The rabbi welcomed him, saying, "Judas. Good, you're here. We've been waiting for you. We couldn't finish the banquet without you" (Jones, 90).

? Questions for Reflection

1. Some find this parable, as a story of God's judgment, too challenging or even upsetting. What was your response to the message of this parable? How do you understand the theological idea of judgment?

2. In your opinion, is this parable about invitations or rejections? On whose part? Why?

3. If, in this parable, the wedding garment symbolizes the faithfulness and obedience God expects of those who are members of the kingdom, what "wedding garments" should Christians wear today?

4. One possibility for translating verse 14 might be, "For many are invited, but few are the best." How does this translation affect your understanding of the parable?

The Betrayal and Trial of Jesus

Shortly after the parable of the wedding banquet, Jesus states two commandments that are key to active righteousness: love God with all your heart, soul, and mind; and love your neighbor as yourself (22:37–40). Then follows a grim cycle of a denunciation of the scribes and Pharisees, a lament over Jerusalem, and the foretelling of the destruction of the Temple (23:1–24:35), which leads into a section on readiness for the kingdom (24:36–25:46). The stage is set for the final days of Jesus.

The Betrayal

Jesus' betrayal by Judas was foretold by Matthew in 17:22–23 and 26:14–16. Now that the dreaded moment has come, Jesus' own actions and teachings command the scene. Rather than being a victim, Jesus is a voluntary agent in a larger plan. He does not wait to be hunted down. Instead, he advances with dignity to meet his betrayer, who greets him with a hypocritical kiss (26:49).

After Judas signals the mob with a kiss, Jesus takes the offensive. He gives Judas an order that reveals his knowledge of how things will go: "Friend, do what you are here to do" (26:50). When one of the disciples arms himself in his defense, Jesus

> **"Kiss of Death"**
>
> Our popular phrase comes from this incident, but also calls to mind Proverbs 27:6. A kiss is used for betrayal in one other place in scripture, 2 Samuel 20:9, where a man proceeds to knife his brother in the belly (a death similar to the description of Judas's own death in Acts 1:18).

does not let the disciple's emotion rule the moment. He refuses to use his powers to overcome his enemies with violence. Rather, he commands his disciple to put the sword away (26:52) and acknowledges that he will go along with the scheme of the scriptures (26:53–54).

Then Jesus defines the situation. He states for all to hear that he is not a criminal. He refuses to be caricatured as a guerrilla revolutionary or one who steals to fund his cause (26:55). Again, so that the scriptures will be fulfilled, Jesus does not desert the plan, though his disciples desert him (26:56). Jesus must face these last hours of humiliation and suffering alone.

The Trial of Jesus

The trial of Jesus, as recounted by all four Gospels, raises many questions: What was the charge? What made that charge punishable by death? Which group had primary responsibility for Jesus' death? John's Gospel depicts Roman authorities and Jewish leaders working together from the outset to bring about Jesus' death. Jesus is crucified both as a political threat to the Romans and as an embarrassment to the Jews. John's Gospel explicitly states that the Sanhedrin (the Jewish Court) did not have the power to inflict the death sentence (John 18:31).

The other three Gospels (especially Mark and Matthew) emphasize the proceedings of the Jewish court. Matthew's account includes a dramatic hand-washing scene in which Pilate leaves the Jews fully responsible for the outcome. Matthew's account also is problematic because the legal proceedings do not seem to concur with what is known historically of the procedure in the Jewish courts of Jesus' day. In trying capital cases, the Sanhedrin had to meet in daytime on two consecutive days with private interrogation of witnesses. By contrast, Jesus is taken to the high priest's house *at night* (26:57–58). More than likely, the whole Sanhedrin would not have been assembled in the middle of the night, especially the night before Passover. Perhaps what took place was an informal inquiry by the Sadducean priests—a meeting before Caiaphas, after which Jesus was taken to Pilate.

Jesus before the High Priest

Clearly, Matthew's Gospel attempts to make the Jews responsible for the execution of their Messiah. Both the Markan and Matthean accounts of the trial reflect the situation in the second half of the first century, when tension between the budding church and established Judaism ran high. The early church, which was seeking establishment in the Roman Empire, tended to minimize the involvement of the Roman authorities in their Savior's death. However, Jesus' death by crucifixion shows that the formal trial and sentence were the work of a Roman court because crucifixion was a Roman penalty.

In 26:65, Caiaphas charges Jesus with blasphemy. The crime of blasphemy meant that Jesus had cursed or insulted God or God's name (see Ex. 22:28; Lev. 24:16). How narrowly blasphemy was defined in Jesus' day, and what penalty could be imposed, is unknown. From the synoptic accounts of the trial, blasphemy apparently did not merit punishment by death in Roman courts. Because the Romans would not tolerate political insurgence, the religious authorities focused on the political implications of Jesus' messianic claims. The trouble was that Jesus had not claimed to be the Messiah and indeed had told people not to spread that message concerning him (9:30; 16:20; 17:9).

> The office of high priest was a lifetime appointment whose primary role was to act as the mediator between God and the people, and to offer up the sin offering on the Day of Atonement. There is irony in this confrontation between Caiaphas and Jesus, the great High Priest (Heb. 5:1–6).

When the religious authorities racked their brains to remember a time Jesus claimed to be the Messiah, all they could recall was a promise to destroy the Temple and raise it again in three days. It is interesting to note that Jesus makes no such claim in Matthew's Gospel, though he does predict the Temple's destruction (24:2). The charge appears across the Gospels, and John 2:19 does record Jesus making the remark. Still, the meaning of Jesus' statement is unclear. Did Jesus refer to the physical temple of his day? Did he mean he would build a temple in the coming age? Was he describing the community of believers that would be created through his resurrection on the third day? Opinions disagree, but the Sanhedrin saw decidedly a messianic claim in this saying. Only someone who believed himself divine would boast of destroying and rebuilding the Temple in a three-day period. No man could be divine, therefore God was blasphemed.

Caiaphas demands that Jesus corroborate the claim under oath that he is the Messiah. He phrases his question as a clever trap. Caiaphas asks, not, "Have you claimed to be the Messiah in the past?" but rather, "Are you the Messiah?" Jesus offers an ambiguous reply that Matthew clearly intends the reader to understand as a positive response, "You have said so." The affirmation is as if Jesus is saying to Caiaphas, "You are obviously afraid that I might be, or you wouldn't have brought me here. On what grounds are you suspicious that I may be the Messiah?"

"You have said so"

After Jesus' death and resurrection, Jesus' laconic comment "You have said so" challenged the pagan world. Many people were converted to the early Christian movement by the joy they saw in Christians' lives, by the courage with which many went to their death rather than denounce their belief in Christ, and by their countercultural acts of kindness to abandoned infants and the sick and elderly. As the song we sing in church goes, "They'll know we are Christians by our love."

"You have said so" continues to challenge those who have no church affiliation as well as those who take theirs for granted. What makes people suddenly suspicious, suddenly hopeful that Jesus may indeed be the Messiah sent to save them? Maybe we were brought up reciting affirmations of faith in church without giving them much thought. Maybe we reached a crisis in our young adult years and discovered that what we had been confessing with our lips was true in our lives. Maybe we have seen the power of the risen Christ in a community's pulling together in a disaster, or in a healed family relationship, or in an individual's miraculous turnabout. In these mysterious transformations we glimpse a discernible hand. Was that hand that of our Messiah? Let us say so!

In looking for the Messiah's empowerment in the hopeful happenings around us, we are extending Jesus' own functional understanding of his earthly vocation. In Matthew 11:3, John the Baptist's followers come to Jesus and ask him directly if he is the Messiah. He points them to the fact that the blind see, the lame walk, the lepers are cleansed, the deaf hear, the dead are raised, and the poor have good news brought to them (11:5). His person and actions made the claim for him. His healings, his miracles, his teaching with authority, as well as his forgiveness of sins (9:2) all imply a messianic claim. God is indeed with us.

As Caiaphas asks Jesus, "Who are you?" so Jesus earlier (chapter 16) asked Peter, "Who am I?" "Who do people say that the Son of Man is?"(16:13). Peter presents the options: "John the Baptist, Elijah, Jeremiah, or one of the prophets." "But who do you say that I am?" asks Jesus. If we confess Jesus' Lordship with our lips and with our lives, then others can look to us and to our churches and say, "In them we see not just good intentions or human empathy, but we see God at work."

When Jesus replies to Caiaphas's question "Are you the Messiah?" with the terse sentence "You have said so," he implies that the high priest's accusation is actually a confession of faith! The high priest must have been infuriated. After setting a carefully worded question meant to entrap Jesus, Caiaphas had fallen into the trap himself! Jesus then makes a statement that combines two texts that are crucial to early Christian reflection on Jesus' identity: Psalm 110:1 (see also Matt. 22:44) and Daniel 7:13 (see also Matt. 24:30).

> "Then the high priest tore his clothes" (Matt. 26:65). In scripture, tearing one's garments is a visible sign of great remorse, stemming either from grief, a vow taken too lightly, an injustice, a sign of repentance, or a sense of personal conviction of sin. A priest is expressly forbidden to tear his garments (Lev. 10:6; 21:10).

In the future, the Son of Man, vindicated and at God's right hand, would fulfill a judging role for the nations. Some scholars question whether in these verses Jesus was talking about himself or another end-time judge. Given Jesus' habit in Matthew of referring to himself as the Son of Man, hearers and readers would understand Jesus as referring to his own vindication and future judging role. Jesus will be exalted through death and resurrection to take his place at God's side. From there, at the appointed time, he will come to rescue the elect and judge the wicked.

Jesus' own judges then begin to mistreat him in ways that reveal their rejection of his messianic status. A common Jewish belief about the Messiah was that he would possess prophetic powers. To test Jesus and prove by counterexample that he was not the Messiah, the priests slap him and demand that he name who struck him (26:68).

> The procurator was an agent of the Roman government whose job was to look after the affairs of state in the provinces. Sometimes the procurator is referred to as "governor."

Because they probably had power only to accuse, not to sentence and execute, the members of the Sanhedrin send Jesus on to Pilate, the Roman procurator. The capital charges brought against him in the presence of Pilate bristled with political implications. The charge was that he claimed to be "King of the Jews" (27:11, 29, 37).

The main point of this story for Matthew is theological rather than historical. The narrative is shaped by later Christian reflection to make a theological point. For Matthew, the trial represents the ultimate confrontation between Jesus and the official leaders of Israel on the subject of his messianic status. We need to be careful as Christians not to assume, on the basis of Matthew's faith narrative, that the Jewish system of justice was hopelessly corrupt or that we can make historical pronouncements about what the Jews did to Jesus. The role of the Pharisees, for example, is not supported in any other relevant historical text. The Pharisees were creative interpreters of the law. They would not have objected this violently to Jesus on the basis of his interpretation of the Sabbath, his treatment of divorce (5:31–32; 19:1–9), or his stand on purity and food laws (15:1–20).

> **"King of the Jews"**
>
> Outside of the Passion narrative, this phrase appears only in the birth narrative at Matthew 2:2, when the Wise Men come searching for the infant Jesus.

We need to keep in mind that Matthew's whole treatment of the scribes and Pharisees reflects late first-century tensions between church and synagogue projected back into the time of Jesus. Under no circumstances should Matthew's Gospel be used as grounds for generalizing about the contemporary strengths and weaknesses of Judaism. Tensions between church and synagogue in the first century must not be imported into the present time. These are errors in interpretation that culminate in destructive anti-Semitism.

The Last Stages

Throughout the story of Jesus' trial and crucifixion, several people attest to his messianic identity while those around them are denying and deserting him. Emphasized to a greater extent in Luke's Gospel, but still glimpsed in the pages of Matthew, are the women who stood by Jesus. Most often not named, and identified only by their relationship with powerful men, these women commit small, stubborn acts of resistance and loyalty.

The servant-girl in the courtyard of Caiaphas's house demands that Peter confess his loyalty to Jesus publicly (26:69). Pilate's wife honors the truth that comes to her from God in dreams and whispers. Convinced of Jesus' innocence, she seeks to sway her powerful husband (27:15–26). Whereas the male disciples have long since fled (26:56), several women watch and lament Jesus' crucifixion from a distance: Mary Magdalene, Mary the mother of James and Joseph, and the mother of the sons of Zebedee (27:55–56). The path of loyalty to Christ still lies in honoring the still small voice of God within and summoning courage to resist unjust and powerful public systems in persistent, daily ways.

The narrative becomes increasingly ominous. Various people display alternatives to loyalty to Jesus in these last hours. Peter denies him; Judas destroys himself. Pilate makes a futile effort to serve God and mammon simultaneously. He halfheartedly attempts to free Jesus while remaining committed to his primary goal to keep the crowd happy. Pilate offers the crowd a choice between Jesus and Jesus Barabbas, a notorious prisoner. Mark portrays him as a rebel "who had committed murder during the insurrection" (Mark 15:7). Jesus (Joshua) was a common name in the first century. We recall that in Matthew 1:21 the angel told Joseph, "You are to name him Jesus, for he will save his people from their sins."

The crowd is offered a choice: between a Jesus who will save them by violence and a Jesus who will save them by voluntary sacrifice out of radical love for them. The crowd is being tempted, as Jesus was earlier, to choose misuse of power over faith in God. Whereas Jesus overcame this temptation, the crowd now succumbs.

The Gospels tend to let Pilate off the hook with regard to Jesus' death. In the Coptic Church, both Pilate and his wife were eventually canonized! History tells us that Pilate was not afraid to be harsh with revolutionaries (Luke 13:1). Possibly Pilate realized that though Jesus himself was not a genuine threat to Roman rule, he could be used as a figurehead by a revolutionary movement (see John 6:14–15).

Matthew transfers as much of the responsibility as possible from Pilate to the Jewish leaders. The stories of Pilate's

> "I wash my hands in innocence." —Psalm 26:6

wife's dream and Pilate's hand washing are unique to his Gospel. Hand washing was not a rite of purification or innocence in pagan society. Most likely the incident traces its inspiration to several verses from the Hebrew Scriptures (Deut. 21:6–7; Pss. 26:6; 73:13).

For Matthew, as much responsibility as possible for Jesus' crucifixion must be placed at the feet of the Jews. His theological conviction was that Israel as a whole had rejected its Messiah in a final and definitive way, and deserved to be deselected as God's special people. The focus and purpose of verse 25, then, is not an attack on the Jews. Rather, the verses are intended to promote the Gentile mission and the church in which Gentiles now predominate (21:43). The apostle Paul provides an antidote to Matthew's anti-Judaism when he eloquently affirms God's abiding relationship to Israel in Romans 11.

"He handed him over to be crucified" (27:26). Ever faithful and obedient, Jesus upholds the two commandments of 22:37–38. His love for God and his love for neighbor lead him to his death.

Want to Know More?

About canonization? See Donald K. McKim, *Westminster Dictionary of Theological Terms* (Louisville, Ky.: Westminster John Knox Press, 1996), 38; Richard P. McBrien, ed., *The HarperCollins Encyclopedia of Catholicism* (San Francisco: HarperSanFrancisco, 1995), 218–19.

About the Coptic Church? See McKim, *Westminster Dictionary of Theological Terms*, 62; McBrien, *HarperCollins Encyclopedia of Catholicism*, 367–68.

About crucifixion? See Paul J. Achtemeier, ed., *Harper's Bible Dictionary* (San Francisco: Harper & Row, 1985), 194–95.

? Questions for Reflection

1. Matthew's passion story portrays Jesus as faithfully following God's plan, even though the plan must lead to his own death. How would you act if you knew the outcome of your life? What might encourage you to stay true to that course?
2. Some see a similarity between the betrayal and trial of Jesus and the temptation story (4:1–11). What are some of the similarities and differences between the two episodes?
3. A variety of characters have their chance in the story of Jesus' betrayal and trial. Some watch from a distance, some wash their hands, some cry for the revolutionary, some can only follow. If you were one of the characters, what might your response have been? Why?
4. The fulfillment of the scriptures is very important to Matthew, and is mentioned at least three times in this passage. To what do those references refer? As our study nears the end of Jesus' life, what are some of the other ways the scriptures have been fulfilled in the life and ministry of Jesus?

Jesus' Death and Resurrection

The story of the crucifixion and death of Jesus must be carefully distinguished from accounts of the glorious deaths of martyrs. In those accounts, the last words of the martyr are uplifting statements of undying faith despite the physical torture the martyr is enduring. In Matthew's account of Jesus' crucifixion, Jesus' last words are "My God, my God, why have you forsaken me?" (27:46; see Ps. 22:1). Troubling to commentators, this verse, taken at face value, depicts Jesus' life ending with a naked display of his humanity, with profound anguish of mind and spirit.

One of the suggested sites of Golgotha—the Place of the Skull

The Cry from the Cross

There are three major streams of interpretation of this verse. The first interpretation theorizes that though Jesus was quoting the first verse of Psalm 22, he intended to imply the whole psalm. Psalm 22 ends on the triumphant note of the psalmist's faith in God's deliverance being spread throughout the entire world. Some evidence exists that some Jews used the opening words of this psalm in this way, and the triumphant climax of the psalm served as a confident prayer for help in time of need. This interpretation flounders because if Psalm 22 was so common a convention, why didn't the crowds recognize Jesus' intentions as such?

A second interpretation of the cry from the cross goes to the other extreme and theorizes that the cry represents a complete loss of faith on Jesus' part. In his last moments, Jesus reflected on his own life and concluded that he was a total failure. The evidence of Jesus' life as depicted in Matthew's Gospel argues to the contrary. Even up to the arrest in Gethsemane and his challenging responses during his trial, Jesus remains a model of faithfulness. What we know of Jesus' faith argues against this theory. In addition, given Matthew's faith and purposes, he would never have included a shout of definitive, bitter despair in the Gospel.

There is a third, more plausible interpretation of Jesus' cry from the cross. This interpretation places the cry firmly within Israel's tradition of righteous sufferers who, on the basis of their faith foundation, question God. This is Job's stance toward God in his own suffering (Job 9:13–35), as well as Qohelet's as he observed that of the oppressed poor (Eccl. 5:8). Throughout the Psalter, righteous sufferers question God's apparent absence and long for God's presence.

Throughout the psalms people long for the constant assurance of God's presence, for a consistent vision of God's face. But though always present, the face of God cannot always be seen. There are enemies to confront and sorrows to endure. God offers ultimate victory and salvation, and many psalms, like Psalm 22, move from questioning to assurance. But in between there are tears to be shed on our couches in the depths of the night. While enemies are encamped round about, there is an apparently unresponsive God to call to task.

The righteous sufferer's rebuke comes out of faith, not out of a lack of faith. The expectation is that God will be present. We don't accuse someone of standing us up whom we never expected to show up in the first place. People who don't believe in God don't bother to rebuke God when they don't feel God near.

For a more thorough understanding of Psalm 22, see Jerome F. D. Creach, *Psalms,* Interpretation Bible Studies (Louisville, Ky.: Geneva Press, 1998).

The depth of the psalmists' faith produces the almost embarrassing depths of their anguish. Their anguish at times makes us wince like we do when we open a door and catch someone in a private moment of grief. We gently close the door and retreat, thinking, "This is not for my ears. I won't intrude." The roughness of the psalmists' outrage abrades our emotions; the brusqueness of their demands of God startles our sense of respect.

Human like Us

This kind of honesty is all very well for the psalmists, we may say, but we'd expect more from the Son of God! We don't expect to hear the Son of God saying, "My God, my God, why have you forsaken me?" That sounds like something we would say. For him to have said something like that would mean that he was human like us. That would mean he had a human body, human emotions, and human experiences.

Of course, since the Council of Nicaea and on the basis of the biblical witness, Christians have insisted that Jesus was fully human as well as fully divine. But many people have trouble embracing Jesus' full humanity—perhaps because humanity is simply difficult to embrace, within ourselves or in others.

> "Here we see Jesus plumbing the uttermost depths of the human situation, so that there might be no place that we might go where he has not been before." —William Barclay, *The Gospel of Matthew*, Daily Study Bible, vol. 2, p. 369.

The human condition is so untidy, both emotionally and physically. The frailty of the human condition has sounds and smells that are not socially acceptable.

We feel awkward when we discover the humanity of those we know. A confused moment, an ill-chosen word, a disorganized office, tardiness for an appointment—all can fill us with uneasiness or discomfort. We are disquieted that we have discovered their imperfection; perhaps they don't have absolute power or control after all. We are embarrassed and ashamed, for we feel we have violated a level of intimacy, only to realize that they are people like us.

People sometimes talk about wanting their ministers to be "down to earth." This desire sounds like the refrain chanted by the crowd in the game of limbo as the bar is lowered and the next contestants step up for their turn: "How low can they go?" That's a question worth pondering, because people don't want their ministers to be too far down to earth! We may want an occasional pulpit anecdote that shows us that they are human, but we probably don't want to know that they struggle with their lives as much as we do with ours.

We are uncomfortable confronting the raw emotions that are part of what makes us human. We want the game face, with only implied pain in the background. We don't want to be there to see our recently widowed friend's shoulders shaking with sobs at midnight. We want to hear her say instead, "I'm coping pretty well with all of this, thanks." We don't want to see the defeated Olympic athlete with his head in his hands, pulling on his hair and bemoaning his failed dream. We want a peppy one-liner at the microphone about how "There's always next time!"

The physicality of the cross is bad enough—Jesus' human body torn and tortured, oozing blood and sweat. Jesus' last words from the cross in Matthew force us to face his torn and tortured emotions as well. As human beings, like the psalmists, we struggle with the apparent absence of God when we need God most. So did Jesus. At times we assume that if we do not feel God present, God is not present. So did Jesus. The irony of Jesus' question in Matthew is that in the very situation that seems to negate all faith, God had never been closer: "In Christ God was reconciling the world to himself" (2 Cor. 5:19).

> "This is not a Hollywood movie where the good guys never die; this is the story of Jesus the Messiah who must 'undergo great suffering . . . and be killed.' (Matt. 16:21)." —Thomas G. Long, *Matthew*, Westminster Bible Companion, 318.

In his anguished, very human cry from the cross, Jesus puts his own teachings to the test. "Blessed are the poor in spirit (those who know their need of God), for theirs is the kingdom of heaven." The resurrection is God's answer to Jesus' cry from the cross, the divine response to Good Friday. Jesus' struggle to be obedient to the point of death, which we observe at Gethsemane (26:39), is honored by God. The righteous one is vindicated. The resurrection is the lens through which disciples then and now view the cross. Only with the resurrection can we understand Jesus' death, the crucifixion of the Messiah, as a triumph rather than a tragedy.

There is a mysterious irony that God indeed was closest to Jesus in the moments of apparent absence on the cross. Through Christ's presence in our lives today, we can claim that irony at the pain points of our own experience. The crucifixion and the resurrection together witness to a powerful piece of good news. The reconciling, light-bearing God is never closer to us than during those times when we demand to know why God has stood us up. In our suffering, the resurrected Jesus is our best teacher. In our time of need, our risen Lord is our very present help. In tough times, our emotional state may fluctuate from anger to despair to hope. The steady reality of the resurrection grounds us—mind, heart, and body—in the knowledge of a God whose love is stronger than death.

Even in the midst of the reality of death, God is present, pointing to the reality of life. Author Madeleine L'Engle describes this reality: "The summer my husband was dying, and I knew he was dying, I never felt closer to God. This is something I cannot explain. It was there. That summer, we ate out on the terrace. Night after night, there were the most gorgeous sunsets. There hasn't been a summer of sunsets like that since. God just laid on these sunsets for us" (Risher, 38).

The Empty Tomb

Matthew's version of Jesus' death plumbs the depths of his human pain and suffering. So Matthew's version of the empty tomb narrative scales the heights of the majesty and power of God in raising Jesus. An earthquake accompanies the angel's arrival in Matthew, and the angel's actions are dramatically described—rolling back the stone and sitting on it. Thus the angel thwarts the plans of Jesus' enemies to hem him in by sealing the tomb and setting the guard around it. The details about the Roman guard are unique to Matthew. The affirmation of these hostile witnesses is clearly intended to make the story more credible to any detractors; even the Romans admit the tomb is empty.

The traditional site of the empty tomb

To scientifically trained people, like many today, no matter how many angels or guards give witness, this scene is difficult to process. The resurrection is not something that can be proved with visual, audible evidence, the way we are used to proving everything else in our "seeing is believing," "what you see is what you get" culture. To complicate matters, the four evangelists, when put on the witness stand, do not even have their stories synchronized. They disagree as to who first discovered the empty tomb, how and when the stone was rolled from the mouth of the tomb, and how many angels were present.

This story is not one to be proven before a jury. "The empty tomb is presented not as a proof, but as a sign of the resurrection" (Hare, 329). This story is meant to be believed rather than proven. It is a faith story. The truth of the empty tomb, and the resurrection to which it points, is tested in the crucibles of our lives. There we dare to believe the news that is too good to be true. When human sin wrecks its worst havoc, our gracious, righteous God can resurrect life and hope in the depths of our lives and communities.

In Matthew's portrayal of the event, Jesus' resurrection ushers in a new era, the beginning of the end-time general resurrection of the dead (1 Cor. 15:20–21). We reveal that new era when our lives are signs of the resurrection. We can never prove the reality of the resurrection to someone else. But our faith can show forth signs of Jesus' dynamic presence in our lives. The truth of the resurrection is made manifest in those who live "as if . . ." Are we living each day as if God is working to bring good from evil, hope from despair, life from death? Are we living as if God can bring justice to the oppressed? Are we living as if we understand God's blessing on our lives?

We are blessed to become blessings to others as we spread the good news through our words and lives, so that people around us say, "You remind us of Jesus Christ, whom we thought was dead." There is a church in Oakland, California, that titles its annual Good Friday service: "Gospel Women: Last at the Cross, First at the Tomb." This sums up the role women played in standing by Jesus and spreading the good news that their risen Lord now stood by them.

The mention of women in the resurrection narrative would have raised the eyebrows of the hearers. For more about women in the times of Jesus, see Carol A. Newsom and Sharon H. Ringe, eds., *Women's Bible Commentary*, expanded ed. (Louisville, Ky.: Westminster John Knox Press, 1998), 482–88; or, see Evelyn and Frank Stagg, *Woman in the World of Jesus* (Philadelphia: Westminster Press, 1978), 215–19.

Why are women depicted as the first to hear and spread the good news that Jesus had been raised from the dead? Women were not viewed as credible witnesses in Jewish courts of Jesus' day. Their inclusion in the story would not have added to its credibility and prestige in the eyes of original readers.

These women must have played an invaluable part in witnessing to the power of God in raising God's Son, both initially and as the early movement matured. The community preserved the accounts of their courageous ministries for future generations. There is a message here for all who view themselves or are viewed by others as unworthy or unlikely messengers of Christ—Christ chooses you!

Catherine Booth, co-founder of the Salvation Army in the 1860s with her husband, William, was a powerful preacher in a time when a woman preacher was viewed by most people as a contradiction in terms. She believed that women should be allowed to preach but, as the wife of a Methodist minister, had not yet preached herself. And then in 1860 she had the following experience:

> As her husband William finished his sermon, she stood up in front of a crowd of more than a thousand packed into Bethesda Chapel and began to speak. Catherine later recalled her inner feelings that morning: "It seemed as if a voice said to me, 'Now if you were to go and testify, you know I would bless it to your own soul as well as to the souls of the people.' I gasped and said in my soul, 'I cannot do it,' and the devil said, 'Besides, you are not prepared to speak. You will look like a fool and have nothing to say.'" Her first words when she rose to speak were, "I want to say a word. . . ." William was as surprised as anyone when she made her sudden announcement, but he quickly recovered, and when she had finished, he announced that she would preach that evening. (Bramwell-Booth, 185; as cited in Smith, 12)

Making Disciples

When the women encounter the risen Christ, he tells them that he will meet the disciples in Galilee. At that meeting, where Matthew ends his Gospel, Jesus offers the disciples his last earthly words. We call them the Great Commission. These words are so popular that some of them are often written over the exits of churches, "Go therefore and make disciples of all nations, baptizing them in the name of the Father and of the Son and of the Holy Spirit" (28:19).

The command to make disciples of all nations is most likely a corrective to 10:5, where Jesus' followers are told to "Go nowhere among the Gentiles, . . . but go rather to the lost sheep of the house of Israel." By Matthew's time, several decades after Jesus' death, the mission to Israel seemed to be slowing to a standstill. The Great Commission turns the church's attention to the Gentile mission, without excluding Jews. It is significant that Matthew both begins and closes the Gospel by emphasizing outreach to the Gentiles in world mission.

The focus of this discipling is teaching, like Jesus' revived interpretation of the existing Torah. Jesus' words continue to specify the focus of the discipling activity. His followers are to go out, "teaching them to obey everything that I have commanded you"(28:20). The Commission doesn't emphasize the need for faith, perhaps because Matthew's assessment of the missionaries' strengths and their potential converts' needs.

> And now the teacher asks his followers to be teachers also.

Matthew is confident that the missionaries will proclaim the good news and summon hearers to faith. Matthew wants to be sure that their converts take Jesus' moral teachings seriously. At the messianic banquet there will be many who have committed their lives to active obedience to their host. Mingling with them, Matthew suspects, will be many who have not bothered to don their wedding garments (22:11–14). Barren trees will be interspersed with fruitful ones. Goats will be mingling with the sheep, and weeds will be competing for ground with the wheat. The missionaries' task, our task, is crucial—to teach and embody Jesus' code of life with urgency and yet with meekness. This is the commission of the church that would be obedient to Christ; it can be accomplished only by those who are poor in spirit—who know their need of God. In asking, seeking, and knocking, Matthew assures us that we will be equipped and strengthened for this task.

A week before Easter 1995, an arson fire ravaged Butler Chapel AME Church in Orangeburg, South Carolina. The elders stood around the charred debris looking at one another in disbelief. Over the next two years volunteers from around the country came to help the members rebuild. In December 1997, they held the first service in their new building. The old church building was a small white frame building at the end of a dirt road. The new version was in a better location, had a nave that seated three hundred people, a new education wing, and a state-of-the-art kitchen. The congregation asked Pastor

 Want to Know More?

About the ages or eras? See William Barclay, *New Testament Words* (Philadelphia: Westminster Press, 1975), 33–41.

About the Council of Nicaea? See Donald K. McKim, *Westminster Dictionary of Theological Terms* (Louisville, Ky.: Westminster John Knox Press, 1996), 188; Richard P. McBrien, ed., *The HarperCollins Encyclopedia of Catholicism* (San Francisco: HarperSanFrancisco, 1995), 916–17.

Jenkins, from First Baptist Church in Bristol, Pennsylvania, whose work crews had helped with the rebuilding, to preach the inaugural sermon. He did not spend the bulk of that sermon congratulating the people for their hard work in rebuilding. Instead, he focused on the church and the call to discipleship. He ended his sermon with these words: "You have an elegant new facility here. The question God has for you today is this: what are you going to do with it?"

Matthew would have us live together in communities shaped by Jesus' teachings about radical righteousness, pure in heart and hungering for the time when God's righteousness will be established for all members of society. He would have us share Jesus' teachings, as Jesus himself did, by example as well as by word. He would have us be about the business of doing. He would have us be strengthened by the presence of our risen, exalted Lord.

For that reason, Matthew begins and ends his Gospel with good news that makes all the difference in the world today. From the beginning and throughout the Gospel, the importance placed on the name of Jesus—Emmanuel, God with us—has been noted. The importance of God's abiding presence in Christ is the final note of this Gospel and is the best news yet: "And remember, I am with you always, to the end of the age" (28:20).

 ## Questions for Reflection

1. In Matthew 27:54, a Roman centurion testifies that Jesus is God's Son. There is irony: it is only in Jesus' death that some come to know what he lived his life trying to communicate. What are other examples of irony in this passage?
2. The resurrection can seem incredible, if not impossible, to our scientific minds. What are some images you can use to explain resurrection to someone who is not familiar with Matthew's Gospel?
3. In the Great Commission, we are commanded to make disciples. What does it mean to be, and to make, a disciple?
4. The Gospel of Matthew begins and ends with the statement about God's presence with us. What are ways you experience God's presence?

Bibliography

Alter, Robert, and Frank Kermode, eds. *The Literary Guide to the Bible.* Cambridge: Harvard University Press, 1987.

Argyle, A. W. *The Cambridge Bible Commentary on the New English Bible.* Cambridge: Cambridge University Press, 1982.

Barclay, William. *The Gospel of Matthew.* 2 vols. Daily Study Bible. Philadelphia: Westminster Press, 1975.

Bonhoeffer, Dietrich. *The Cost of Discipleship.* New York: Macmillan Co., 1960.

Bramwell-Booth, Catherine. Catherine Booth: *The Story of Her Loves.* London: Hodder & Stoughton, 1970.

Bruner, Frederick Dale. *Matthew,* vol. 1: *The Christbook: Matthew 1–12.* Dallas, Tex.: Word, 1987.

Buttrick, George Arthur, ed. *The Interpreter's Dictionary of the Bible.* 4 vols. Nashville: Abingdon Press, 1962. Supplementary volume, ed. Keith Crim, 1975.

Camp, Claudia V. *Wisdom and the Feminine in the Book of Proverbs.* Sheffield, England: Almond Press, 1985.

Edelman, Marian Wright. *The Measure of Our Success: A Letter to My Children and Yours.* Boston: Beacon Press, 1992.

Fenhagen, James C. *More than Wanderers: Spiritual Disciplines for Christian Ministry.* New York: Seabury Press, 1978.

Hare, Douglas R. A. *Matthew.* Interpretation: A Bible Commentary for Teaching and Preaching. Louisville, Ky.: John Knox Press, 1993.

Hill, David. *The Gospel of Matthew.* The New Century Bible Commentary. Grand Rapids: Wm. B. Eerdmans Publishing Co., 1972.

Jones, Alan. *Passion for Pilgrimage: Notes for the Journey Home, Meditations on the Easter Mystery.* San Francisco: Harper & Row, 1989.

Kittel, G., and G. Friedrich, eds. *Theological Dictionary of the New Testament.* Abridged in one volume by Geoffrey Bromiley. Grand Rapids: Wm. B. Eerdmans Publishing Co., 1985.

Levine, Amy-Jill. "Matthew." In *The Women's Bible Commentary,* ed. Carol A. Newsom and Sharon H. Ringe. Louisville Ky.: Westminster John Knox Press, 1992.

Lewis, C. S. *The Screwtape Letters.* London: Fontana Books, 1942.

Long, Thomas G. *Matthew*. Westminster Bible Companion. Louisville, Ky.: Westminster John Knox Press, 1997.

Luz, Ulrich. *New Testament Theology: The Gospel of Matthew*. Cambridge: Cambridge University Press, 1993.

Nouwen, Henri J. M. *The Way of the Heart: Desert Spirituality and Contemporary Ministry*. New York: Seabury Press, 1981.

Peck-Stahl, Heather. "Witnesses." *The Interpreter Magazine*, April 1998, p. 25.

Perrin, Norman. *The New Testament: An Introduction*. New York: Harcourt Brace Jovanovich, 1974.

Risher, Dee Dee. "Listening to the Story: A Conversation with Madeleine L'Engle." *The Other Side*, March–April 1998, p. 38.

Sample, Tex. *Hard Living People and Mainstream Christians*. Nashville: Abingdon Press, 1993.

Schweizer, Eduard. *The Good News according to Matthew*. Atlanta: John Knox Press, 1975.

Smith, Robin. "Celebrating the Leadership of Women: Uncovering Their History." *Connection* 8 (1995): 12.

Stagg, Evelyn, and Frank Stagg. *Woman in the World of Jesus*. Philadelphia: Westminster Press, 1978.

Stookey, Laurence Hull. *Baptism: Christ's Act in the Church*. Nashville: Abingdon Press, 1982.

Wesley, John. *The Journal of John Wesley*. Chicago: Moody Press, 1987.

Williams, James G. "Paraenesis, Excess, and Ethics: Matthew's Rhetoric in the Sermon on the Mount," *Semeia* 50 (1990): 173–74.

Wright, Wendy M. *The Rising: Living the Mysteries of Lent, Easter, and Pentecost*. Nashville: Upper Room Books, 1994.

Interpretation Bible Studies Leader's Guide

Interpretation Bible Studies (IBS), for adults and older youth, are flexible, attractive, easy-to-use, and filled with solid information about the Bible. IBS helps Christians discover the guidance and power of the scriptures for living today. Perhaps you are leading a church school class, a mid-week Bible study group, or a youth group meeting, or simply using this in your own personal study. Whatever the setting may be, we hope you find this *Leader's Guide* helpful. Since every context and group is different, this *Leader's Guide* does not presume to tell you how to structure Bible study for your situation. Instead, the *Leader's Guide* seeks to offer choices—a number of helpful suggestions for leading a successful Bible study using IBS.

> "The church that no longer hears the essential message of the Scriptures soon ceases to understand what it is for and is open to be captured by the dominant religious philosophy of the moment." —James D. Smart, *The Strange Silence of the Bible in the Church: A Study in Hermeneutics* (Philadelphia: Westminster Press, 1970), 10.

How Should I Teach IBS?

1. Explore the Format.

There is a wealth of information in IBS, perhaps more than you can use in one session. In this case, more is better. IBS has been designed to give you a well-stocked buffet of content and teachable insights. Pick and choose what suits your group's needs. Perhaps you will want to split units into two or more sessions, or combine units into a single session. Perhaps you will decide to use only a portion of a

"The more we bring to the Bible, the more we get from the Bible." —William Barclay, *A Beginner's Guide to the New Testament* (Louisville, Ky.: Westminster John Knox Press, 1995), vii.

unit and then move on to the next unit. *There is not a structured theme or teaching focus to each unit that must be followed for IBS to be used.* Rather, IBS offers the flexibility to adjust to whatever suits your context.

A recent survey of both professional and volunteer church educators revealed that their number one concern was that Bible study materials be teacher-friendly. IBS is, indeed teacher-friendly in two important ways. First, since IBS provides abundant content and a flexible design, teachers can shape the lessons creatively, responding to the needs of the group and employing a wide variety of teaching methods. Second, those who wish more specific suggestions for planning the sessions can find them at the Geneva Press web site on the Internet (**www.ppcpub.org**). Search under the keyword "Interpretation Bible Studies" to discover teaching suggestions for each IBS unit as well as helpful quotations, selections from Bible dictionaries and encyclopedias, and other teaching helps.

IBS is also not only teacher-friendly, it is also discussion-friendly. Given the opportunity, most adults and young people relish the chance to talk about the kind of issues raised in IBS. The secret, then, is to determine what works with your group, what will get them to talk. Several good methods for stimulating discussion are presented in this *Leader's Guide,* and once you learn your group, you can apply one of these methods and get the group discussing the Bible and its relevance in their lives.

The format of every IBS unit consists of several features:

a. Body of the Unit. This is the main content, consisting of interesting and informative commentary on the passage and scholarly insight into the biblical text and its significance for Christians today.

b. Sidebars. These are boxes that appear scattered throughout the body of the unit, with maps, photos, quotations, and intriguing ideas. Some sidebars can be identified quickly by a symbol, or icon, that helps the reader know what type of information can be found in that sidebar. There are icons for illustrations, key terms, pertinent quotes, and more.

c. Want to Know More? Each unit includes a "Want to Know

More?" section that guides learners who wish to dig deeper and consult other resources. If your church library does not have the resources mentioned, you can look up the information in other standard Bible dictionaries, encyclopedias, and handbooks, or you can find much of this information at the Geneva Press Web site (see page 112).

d. Questions for Reflection. The unit ends with questions to help the learners think more deeply about the biblical passage and its pertinence for today. These questions are provided as examples only, and teachers are encouraged both to develop their own list of questions and to gather questions from the group. These discussion questions do not usually have specific "correct" answers. Again, the

> "The trick is to make the Bible our book."
> —Duncan S. Ferguson, *Bible Basics: Mastering the Content of the Bible* (Louisville, Ky.: Westminster John Knox Press, 1995), 3.

flexibility of IBS allows you to use these questions at the end of the group time, at the beginning, interspersed throughout, or not at all.

2. Select a Teaching Method.

Here are ten suggestions. The format of IBS allows you to choose what direction you will take as you plan to teach. Only you will know how your lesson should best be designed for your group. Some adult groups prefer the lecture method, while others prefer a high level of free ranging discussion. Many youth groups like interaction, activity, the use of music, and the chance to talk about their own experiences and feelings. Here is a list of a few possible approaches. Let your own creativity add to the list!

a. Let's Talk about What We've Learned. In this approach, all group members are requested to read the scripture passage and the IBS unit before the group meets. Ask the group members to make notes about the main issues, concerns, and questions they see in the passage. When the group meets, these notes are collected, shared, and discussed. This method depends, of course, on the group's willingness to do some "homework."

b. What Do We Want and Need to Know? This approach begins by having the whole group read the scripture passage together.

Then, drawing from your study of the IBS, you, as the teacher, write on a board or flip chart two lists:

(1) Things we should know to better understand this passage" (content information related to the passage, for example, historical insights about political contexts, geographical landmarks, economic nuances, etc.] and

(2) Four or five "important issues we should talk about regarding this passage" [with implications for today- how the issues in the biblical context continue into today, for example, issues of idolatry or fear]. Allow the group to add to either list, if they wish, and use the lists to lead into a time of learning, reflection, and discussion. This approach is suitable for those settings where there is little or no advanced preparation by the students.

> "Although small groups can meet for many purposes and draw upon many different resources, the one resource which has shaped the life of the Church more than any other throughout its long history has been the Bible." —Roberta Hestenes, *Using the Bible in Groups* (Philadelphia: Westminster Press, 1983), 14.

c. Hunting and Gathering. Start the unit by having the group read the scripture passage together. Then divide the group into smaller clusters (perhaps having as few as one person), each with a different assignment. Some clusters can discuss one or more of the "Questions for Reflection." Others can look up key terms or people in a Bible dictionary or track down other biblical references found in the body of the unit. After the small clusters have had time to complete their tasks, gather the entire group again and lead them through the study material, allowing each cluster to contribute what it learned.

d. From Question Mark to Exclamation Point. This approach begins with contemporary questions and then moves to the biblical content as a response to those questions. One way to do this is for you to ask the group, at the beginning of the class, a rephrased version of one or more of the "Questions for Reflection" at the end of the study unit. For example, one of the questions at the end of the unit on Exodus 3:1–4:17 in the IBS *Exodus* volume reads,

Moses raised four protests, or objections, to God's call. Contemporary people also raise objections to God's call. In what ways are these similar to Moses' protests? In what ways are they different?

This question assumes familiarity with the biblical passage about

Moses, so the question would not work well before the group has explored the passage. However, try rephrasing this question as an opening exercise; for example:

> Here is a thought experiment: Let's assume that God, who called people in the Bible to do daring and risky things, still calls people today to tasks of faith and courage. In the Bible, God called Moses from a burning bush and called Isaiah in a moment of ecstatic worship in the Temple. How do you think God's call is experienced by people today? Where do you see evidence of people saying "yes" to God's call? When people say "no" or raise an objection to God's call, what reasons do they give (to themselves, to God)?

Posing this or a similar question at the beginning will generate discussion and raise important issues, and then it can lead the group into an exploration of the biblical passage as a resource for thinking even more deeply about these questions.

e. Let's Go to the Library.   From your church library, your pastor's library, or other sources, gather several good commentaries on the book of the Bible you are studying. Among the trustworthy commentaries are those in the Interpretation series (John Knox Press) and the Westminster Bible Companion series (Westminster John Knox Press). Divide your group into smaller clusters and give one commentary to each cluster (one or more of the clusters can be given the IBS volume instead of a full-length commentary). Ask each cluster to read the biblical passage you are studying and then to read the section of the commentary that covers that passage (if your group is large, you may want to make photocopies of the commentary material with proper permission, of course). The task of each cluster is to name the two or three most important insights they discover about the biblical passage by reading and talking together about the commentary material. When you reassemble the larger group to share these insights, your group will not only gain a variety of insights about the passage but also a sense that differing views of the same text are par for the course in biblical interpretation.

f. Working Creatively Together.   Begin with a creative group task, tied to the main thrust of the study. For example, if the study is on the Ten Commandments, a parable, or a psalm, have the group rewrite the Ten Commandments, the parable, or the psalm in contemporary language. If the passage is an epistle, have the group write a letter to their own congregation. Or if the study is a narrative, have the group role-play the characters in the story or write a page describing the story from the point of view of one of the characters. After completion of the task, read and discuss the biblical passage, asking for interpretations and applications from the group and tying in IBS material as it fits the flow of the discussion.

g. Singing Our Faith. Begin the session by singing (or reading) together a hymn that alludes to the biblical passage being studied (or to the theological themes in the passage). Most hymnals have an index of scriptural allusions. For example, if you are studying the unit from the IBS volume on Psalm 121, you can sing "I to the Hills Will Lift My Eyes," "Sing Praise to God, Who Reigns Above," or another hymn based on Psalm 121. Let the group reflect on the thoughts and feelings evoked by the hymn, then move to the biblical passage, allowing the biblical text and the IBS material to underscore, clarify, refine, and deepen the discussion stimulated by the hymn. If you are ambitious, you may ask the group to write a new hymn at the end of the study! [Many hymnals have indexes in the back or companion volumes that help the user match hymns to scripture passages or topics.]

h. Fill in the Blanks. In order to help the learners focus on the content of the biblical passage, at the beginning of the session ask each member of the group to read the biblical passage and fill out a brief questionnaire about the details of the passage (provide a copy for each learner or write the questions on the board). For example, if you are studying the unit in the IBS *Matthew* volume on Matthew 22:1–14, the questionnaire could include questions such as the following:

—In this story, Jesus compares the kingdom of heaven to what?
—List the various responses of those who were invited to the king's banquet but who did not come.
—When his invitation was rejected, how did the king feel? What did the king do?
—In the second part of the story, when the king saw a man at the banquet without a wedding garment, what did the king say? What did the man say? What did the king do?
—What is the saying found at the end of this story?

Gather the group's responses to the questions perhaps encourage discussion. Then lead the group through the IBS material helping the learners to understand the meanings of these details and the significance of the passage for today. Feeling creative? Instead of a fill-in-the blanks questionnaire, create a crossword puzzle from names and words in the biblical passage.

i. Get the Picture. In this approach, stimulate group discussion by incorporating a painting, photograph, or other visual object into the lesson. You can begin by having the group examine and comment on this visual or you can introduce the visual later in the lesson—it depends on the object used. If, for example, you are studying the unit Exodus 3:1–4:17 in the IBS *Exodus* volume, you may want to view Paul Koli's very colorful painting *The Burning Bush*. Two sources for this painting are *The Bible Through Asian Eyes*, edited by Masao Takenaka and Ron O'Grady (National City, Calif.: Pace Publishing Co., 1991), and *Imaging the Word: An Arts and Lectionary Resource*, vol. 3, edited by Susan A. Blain (Cleveland: United Church Press, 1996).

j. Now Hear This. Especially if your class is large, you may want to use the lecture method. As the teacher, you prepare a presentation on the biblical passage, using as many resources as you have available plus your own experience, but following the content of the IBS unit as a guide. You can make the lecture even more lively by asking the learners at various points along the way to refer to the visuals and quotes found in the "sidebars." A place can be made for questions (like the ones at the end of the unit)— either at the close of the lecture or at strategic points along the way.

> "It is . . . important to call a Bible study group back to what the text being discussed actually says, especially when an individual has gotten off on some tangent." —Richard Robert Osmer, *Teaching for Faith: A Guide for Teachers of Adult Classes* (Louisville, Ky.: Westminster John Knox Press, 1992), 71.

3. Keep These Teaching Tips in Mind

There are no surefire guarantees for a teaching success. However, the following suggestions can increase the chances for a successful study:

a. Always Know Where the Group Is Headed. Take ample time beforehand to prepare the material. Know the main points of the study, and know the destination. Be flexible, and encourage discussion, but don't lose sight of where you are headed.

b. Ask Good Questions; Don't Be Afraid of Silence. Ideally, a discussion blossoms spontaneously from the reading of the scripture. But more often than not, a discussion must be drawn from the group members by a series of well-chosen questions. After asking each question, give the group members time to answer. Let them think, and don't be threatened by a season of silence. Don't feel that every question must have an answer, and that as leader, you must supply every answer. Facilitate discussion by getting the group members to cooperate with each other. Sometimes, the original question can be restated. Sometimes it is helpful to ask a follow-up question like "What makes this a hard question to answer?"

Ask questions that encourage explanatory answers. Try to avoid questions that can be answered simply "Yes" or "No." Rather than asking, "Do you think Moses was frightened by the burning bush?" ask, "What do you think Moses was feeling and experiencing as he stood before the burning bush?" If group members answer with just one word, ask a follow-up question like "Why do you think this is so?" Ask questions about their feelings and opinions, mixed within questions about facts or details. Repeat their responses or restate their response to reinforce their contributions to the group.

"Studies of learning reveal that while people remember approximately 10% of what they hear, they remember up to 90% of what they say. Therefore, to increase the amount of learning that occurs, increase the amount of talking about the Bible which each member does."—Roberta Hestenes, *Using the Bible in Groups* (Philadelphia: Westminster Press, 1983), 17.

Most studies can generate discussion by asking open-ended questions. Depending on the group, several types of questions can work. Some groups will respond well to content questions that can be answered from reading the IBS comments or the biblical passage. Others will respond well to questions about feelings or thoughts. Still others will respond to questions that challenge them to new thoughts or that may not have exact answers. Be sensitive to the group's dynamic in choosing questions.

Some suggested questions are: What is the point of the passage? Who are the main characters? Where is the tension in the story? Why does it say (this)_____, and not (that) _____? What raises questions for you? What terms need defining? What are the new ideas? What doesn't make sense? What bothers or troubles you about this passage? What keeps you from living the truth of this passage?

c. Don't Settle for the Ordinary. There is nothing like a surprise. Think of special or unique ways to present the ideas of the study. Upset the applecart of the ordinary. Even though the passage may be familiar, look for ways to introduce suspense. Remember that a little mystery can capture the imagination. Change your routine.

Along with the element of surprise, humor can open up a discussion. Don't be afraid to laugh. A well-chosen joke or cartoon may present the central theme in a way that a lecture would have stymied.

Sometimes a passage is too familiar. No one speaks up because everyone feels that all that could be said has been said. Choose an unfamiliar translation from which to read, or if the passage is from a Gospel, compare the story across two or more Gospels and note differences. It is amazing what insights can be drawn from seeing something strange in what was thought to be familiar.

d. Feel Free to Supplement the IBS Resources with Other Material. Consult other commentaries or resources. Tie in current events with the lesson. Scour newspapers or magazines for stories that touch on the issues of the study. Sometimes the lyrics of a song, or a section of prose from a well-written novel will be just the right seasoning for the study.

e. And Don't Forget to Check the Web. Check out our site on the World Wide Web (keyword "Interpretation Bible Studies" at www.ppcpub.org). Several possibilities for applying the teaching methods suggested above for individual IBS units will be available. Feel free to read, print, or download this material.

f. Stay Close to the Biblical Text. Don't forget that the goal is to learn the Bible. Return to the text again and again. Avoid making the mistake of reading the passage only at the beginning of the study, and then wandering away to comments on top of comments from that point on. Trust in the power and presence of the Holy Spirit to use the truths of the passage to work within the lives of the study participants.

> "The Bible is literature, but it is much more than literature. It is the holy book of Jews and Christians, who find there a manifestation of God's presence." —Kathleen Norris, *The Psalms* (New York: Riverhead Books, 1997), xxii.

What If I Am Using IBS in Personal Bible Study?

If you are using IBS in your personal Bible study, you can experiment and explore a variety of ways. You may choose to read straight through the study without giving any attention to the sidebars or other features. Or you may find yourself interested in a question or unfamiliar with a key term, and you can allow the sidebars," "Want to Know More?" and "Questions for Reflection" to lead you into deeper learning on these issues. Perhaps you will want to have a few commentaries or a Bible dictionary available to pursue what interests you. As was suggested in one of the teaching methods above, you may want to begin with the questions at the end, and then read the Bible passage followed by the IBS material. Trust the IBS resources to provide good and helpful information, and then follow your interests!

Want to Know More?

About leading Bible study groups? See Roberta Hestenes, *Using the Bible in Groups* (Philadelphia: Westminster Press, 1983).

About basic Bible content? See Duncan S. Ferguson, *Bible Basics: Mastering the Content of the Bible* (Louisville, Ky.: Westminster John Knox Press, 1995); William M. Ramsay, *The Westminster Guide to the Books of the Bible* (Louisville, Ky.: Westminster John Knox Press, 1994).

About the development of the Bible? See John Barton, *How the Bible Came to Be* (Louisville, Ky.: Westminster John Knox Press, 1997).

About the meaning of difficult terms? See Donald K. McKim, *Westminster Dictionary of Theological Terms* (Louisville, Ky.: Westminster John Knox Press, 1996); Paul J. Achtemeier, *Harper's Bible Dictionary* (San Francisco: Harper & Row, 1985).

For more information about IBS,

search under the keyword
"Interpretation Bible Studies" at
www.ppcpub.org